VICTUAL LICENCES

Records for Family and Local Historians

Third Edition

Jeremy Gibson

The Family History Partnership

200575766

his edition published 2009 by
Family History Partnership,
PO Box 502,
Bury, Lancashire BL8 9EP

es@thefamilyhistorypartnership.com
www.thefamilyhistorypartnership.com

First edition, 1994.
Second edition, 1997, reprinted (with minor amendments) 2000.
Both published by the Federation of Family History Societies.

Third edition Copyright © Jeremy Gibson, 2009.

ISBN 978 1 906280 14 7

Typeset from computer discs prepared by Jeremy Gibson
and printed by Parchment (Oxford) Limited.

Cover illustration. Detail from Hogarth's "Beer Street", a 'companion' to the famous "Gin Lane". He claimed it was 'a contrast; where that invigorating liquor [beer] is recommended, in order to drive the other [gin] out of vogue. Here all is joyous and thriving. Industry and jollity go hand in hand. In this happy place the pawnbroker's is the only house going to ruin; and even the small quantity of porter he can procure is taken in at the wicket, for fear of further distress.'

ACKNOWLEDGMENTS

This Guide arose out of the late Judith Hunter's work on a thesis for the History Department of Reading University, entitled 'Legislation, Royal Proclamations, and other directives affecting inns, taverns, alehouses, brandy shops and punch houses, 1552-1757'. She allied her considerable historical knowledge of the licensed victualling trade to a tremendous amount of work in gathering, at my suggestion, information on the records it has generated from the sixteenth to the twentieth centuries, now largely housed in local record offices throughout the country. The archivists who are their custodians responded in their normal helpful way to the rather dauntingly long and complex questionnaire we circulated. As always we were then and I still am enormously grateful to them.

My own involvement in the preparation of the first edition of this Guide was more than usually peripheral. However, in later editions I have been able to add details of wine licences, 1626-39, in Lord Keeper Thomas Coventry's papers at Worcestershire Record Office, and, at The National Archives, the 1756 military survey (which in a few areas names licensees and inn signs). For this third edition all record offices were once again circulated, and replies were received from a gratifying number, with considerable addition of recently deposited twentieth century archives.

Once again I am taking the opportunity of including a dedication – to my former next-door neighbours, Lorrie Jones, Steve Chick, and many others, licensees of the *Hand and Shears* (first recorded under this name in 1775 [Oxfordshire Record Office, Victuallers' Recognizances, QSD.V.1]), and all those many licensees whose hospitality I have enjoyed for over seventy years since my first recollected visit to a pub (for tea), the *Trout* at Godstow (where the Mayor of Oxford had lunched in 1625 on his way round the city franchises [*Oxford Council Acts 1583-1626*, ed. H.E. Salter, page 425, ex *V.C.H., Oxon.*, **12**, 1990]).

J.S.W.G.

CONTENTS

INTRODUCTION to the RECORDS

The late Judith Hunter

Licences to sell ale and beer, 1552-1828

The first Act concerned with licensing the sale of intoxicating liquor was passed in 1552. It ordered that all keepers of alehouses and tippling houses should be licensed either by the justices of the peace at the Sessions Court or by two justices out of Sessions, and that from time to time the ale sellers should enter into recognizances, or bonds, that they would maintain good order in their houses and not allow the playing of unlawful games, such a quoits, bowls, cards, dice, football and tennis. This recognizance had to be certified at the Sessions Court and kept on record.

This first Act, modified by various Acts of Parliament, royal proclamations,and orders of Privy Council, remained in force until 1753. It was then replaced by a new Act which 'tidied-up' the legislation, but did not radically change it. The terms of the recognizances, however, had long been extended to include numerous restrictions, the breaking of which could result in a fine or loss of licence. The 1552 Act did not specify the duration of the licence, but within a few years some counties and boroughs were renewing licences annually and in 1619 a royal proclamation ordered that licences were to be issued annually at special licensing sessions. In 1729 annual licensing at Special Licensing or Brewster Sessions was made a statutory requirement, and magistrates were ordered to grant licences only to houses within their division. The regulation of alehouses and their licensees, however, continued to be of county, as well as local, concern, and licensing records may be found in the several classes of records.

Quarter Sessions records

Original Recognizances. The bond made before two justices that the alehouse keeper or other retailer of ale and beer would keep an orderly house. The name of the licensee and his parish are recorded and it is also usual for the names of those that stood surety to be given. The name of the house, or inn sign, is rarely recorded in sixteenth and seventeenth century recognizances, but those of the late eighteenth and early nineteenth centuries often do give the pub name. The recognizances may be kept separately as a recognizance roll, or in bundles, or be bound up with the Sessional Rolls or Files.

Sessional Rolls or Files. As well as the recognizances, these rolls or files may include presentments, petitions and indictments concerning unlicensed alehouse keepers and licensees who broke the conditions of their bonds. There may also be lists or registers of alehouse keepers.

Sessional Order Books. These are the formal records of the proceedings of the Court and may also include records of recognizances, presentments and indictments as well as orders concerning suppression of licensed premises.

Researchers should consult any calendars or transcripts of the Sessions records, where these are available, at the record office or, if published, at major libraries. They will be found listed in the companion Guide to *Quarter Sessions Records*.

Registers of Recognizances or Victuallers' Registers. As early as 1619 clerks of the peace were ordered to keep an annual register of all recognizances, but few seventeenth century registers have survived (or were compiled). However, the 1753 Licensing Act made the keeping such registers a statutory requirement and most counties have some registers dating from the late eighteenth century, if not earlier.

The most detailed registers contain the names of the licensees, the parish, inn sign, the 'occupation' of the victuallers, and the names and occupations of those standing surety. They are usually arranged in licensing districts (or divisions) and within each district by parishes. Middlesex and a few other counties and boroughs began keeping such registers before 1753. They usually cease to be kept after 1828.

Certificates of good character (may be called testimonials). The 1753 Act also required prospective licensees (that is those who were not licensed the previous year) to produce a certificate of good character signed by the minister and churchwardens or other substantial residents. Names of applicants and inn signs are usually given.

Constables' Returns. In the mid-eighteenth century Middlesex magistrates ordered parish constables to make lists of victuallers and spirit retailers because of their concern with the excessive consumption of alcohol, especially spirits. The returns usually give the name of the retailer, whether a victualler or brandy (spirit) retailer, licensed or unlicensed, the inn sign, and sometimes the street name. A few other areas have constables' returns but they may not be concerned with the consumption of spirits.

Petty Sessions records[1]

Surviving Petty Sessions records are rare before the nineteenth century, but those that do survive are likely to contain recognizances, lists of alehouse keepers licensed at Special Sessions, and details of cases concerning unlicensed alehouse keepers and sellers of spirits, and disorderly houses, etc.

Occasionally the journal or papers of an individual clerk or magistrate have survived which contain similar information.

Borough records

Many boroughs were their own licensing authority, holding their own Quarter Sessions and keeping similar records to those of the County Quarter Sessions. However, towns also held other courts, and the relevant records may be with those other courts, such as the Mayor's Court or the Court Leet.

Family and estate papers of men who were justices of the peace occasionally contain both references to licensing matters and individual licensing records.

Assize records

During the sixteenth and seventeenth centuries the assize judges were expected to enquire about licensed and unlicensed alehouses, and difficult cases concerning licensing might reach these courts.

These records have not been included in this Guide.

Parish records

The day to day supervision of alehouses was the task of the parish constable, and he was also responsible for presenting details of both licensed and unlicensed alehouses at Quarter Sessions and Petty Sessions. At various times the Vestry were concerned with the number and character of the alehouse keepers in the parish, and whether or not they were licensed.

These records have not been included in this Guide.[2]

---

1. The most detailed references to early Petty Sessions records and those of individual magistrates are found in *Reform in the Provinces: the government of Stuart England* by Anthony Fletcher.
2. One example is included: see Yorkshire (York): Borthwick Institute.

National records

The question of licensing and the problem of regulating the sale of alcohol was a matter which at various times concerned national government. As a result several different types of records are centrally held at The National Archives and elsewhere.

Victuallers' (Lenten) Recognizances, 1572-1634: TNA [E 180, C 203]. An Act of 1562 prohibited inns, alehouses, taverns and other victualling houses selling or serving meat during Lent and at other prohibited times. As a result innkeepers, alehouse keepers and other victuallers were from time to time required to be bound by recognizance not to serve meat at prohibited times. The licensees' names, places of abode, occupations and the names of their sureties are usually given. Consult the index on the open shelves to get the piece number for your county or town. The recognizances are usually handwritten, on one side in Latin, and on the other in English.

There are also recognizances for the Palatinates of Chester 1580-1640 [CHES 38] and Durham, 1583-4 [DURH 8], and for the City of London, 1593-1641 [C 203/1, C 265].

Occasionally reference to, or examples of, these Lenten victuallers' recognizances are found in Quarter Sessions and borough records.

State Papers Domestic: TNA Office. During the sixteenth and early seventeenth century lists of licensed alehouse keepers or their houses were sometimes required by the Government; these are found amongst the State Papers.[3]

Military Survey 1756: TNA WO.30/49. See note on page 11.

Inn (Mompesson) Licences, 1617 - 1620

Innkeepers were not included in the first licensing law of 1552 though much subsequent legislation regulating alehouses applied to inns as well as alehouses and other victualling houses. Thus many of the above records include inns and innkeepers as retailers of ale, regardless of whether the house was an inn or alehouse.[4]

In 1617, however, Sir Giles Mompesson obtained a patent which authorised him and his agents to license inns (as an inn providing accommodation, not merely selling ale or beer) throughout the country. He so abused the patent that he was impeached by Parliament in 1621, but not before many hundreds of inns had been licensed. The patent was revoked that year, and from 1621 any inn selling ale and beer was required to obtain alehouse licences.

Four of Sir Giles Mompesson's account books survive. One is in the House of Lords Record Office; two are found amongst the Declared Accounts of the Pipe Roll. The fourth and most complete set of accounts is in private hands, but a photocopy of it has been deposited in the Centre for Buckinghamshire Studies [D/X 648]. In all the books the names of the innholders, parish or town, and the inn sign are given. For some periods the date of the licence, the fee paid and the annual 'rent' is also given. The places for which licences were issued in 1620 (which include all the earlier ones) have (for the first time) been abstracted (from the C.B.S. photocopy) for this Guide and are shown under each county. Only a very few original Mompesson licences, for Buckinghamshire and Somerset, are known to exist.

---

3. The *Calendars of State Papers, Domestic* are well indexed and these should be searched first. The calendars, however, do not give the details of licensees' names etc which may be recorded on the originals. Certificate of Inns, Taverns and Alehouses, 1577, gives the number of each in each county, and occasionally (Berks. and Bucks.) the names of licensees/landlords [PRO SP 12]. ***These records have not been included in this Guide.***
4. For differences between the different types of establishment, see the Glossary on pages 61-63.

Taverns and Wine Licences, 1553 - 1792

The first law which required taverners and other retailers of wine to be licensed was passed in 1553. This Act and many subsequent records make it quite clear that taverns could be, and often were, quite separate and different establishments from either inns or alehouses. The law restricted taverns to towns, boroughs and cities and required that the retailers of wine should be nominated by the mayor or other chief officer, and the majority of the council, and should be licensed by them, or if there were no council, by the justices of the peace. However, within a year,Queen Mary was also granting licences by letters patent. In 1570 the Crown granted the privilege to issue wine licences to Edward Horsey. From this date until 1757 wine licences were granted either by royal patentees, or the Crown, directly or through agents or wine commissioners. In 1757 the issuing of wine licences was transferred to the Stamp Office. In 1792 the law was changed and wine licences came under the control of the magistrates, who could only issue them to those already licensed to sell ale and beer. No provision appears to have been made to register these.

Wine Licences by Letters Patent, 1554-1571: these are indexed (under 'wine', 'taverns', or 'licences') in the *Calendars of Patent Rolls,* for the reigns of Queen Mary and Queen Elizabeth. They give the name of the wine retailer, his, her or their place of abode, their present occupation, and length of time for which licence was valid (10 years, 21 years, life etc). Places for which such wine licences were granted, 1554-1571, are shown under each county. None have been found after 1571.

Vintners' fines, 1569-1572, and Informations, 1566/7, 1569/70, 1583-9 [E 176]. The vintners' fines are indentures made between the patentee of wine licences, Sir Edward Horsey, or his agent, Richard Ellis, and the keepers of taverns and other wine retailers for payment of fines for offences against the 1552 Wine Act. The names of the offenders, usually unlicensed retailers or those who had charged above the set price, and their place of abode are usually given. The informations are, as the names suggests, records of information given about offenders. If the retailer was fined, the informer received part of the fine.

Fines and informations are found for wine sellers in most counties except London, Northumberland, the Welsh counties and Monmouthshire. Places named in the calendar are shown under each county section.

Wine licences issued by royal patentees, 1583-1602, c.1603-5, and *1626-39.* The counterparts of wine licences granted by Sir Walter Raleigh, 1583-1602, each sealed by both parties, stamped with Raleigh's signature and signed by the licensee, exist in some quantity [C238]. The individual licences are printed, with the names of the taverner and place of abode added in manuscript; tavern or inn sign are not given. The licences are grouped according to regnal year, 25 Elizabeth I (1582-3) to 44 Elizabeth I (1601-2). They are generally in very bad condition, with a centrally placed string holding each file together, so are very difficult to consult. There is the counterpart of just one Wine Licence c.1603-5, issued by the Earl of Nottingham, for a Devon tavern [E163/17/21].

The official papers of Lord Keeper Thomas Coventry, at Worcestershire Record Office (formerly at Birmingham Central Library), include lists of 604 wine licences issued between 1626 and 1639, naming licensees and location, but not the tavern or inn signs. These have been transcribed, copies available at Birmingham, Worcester and the Society of Genealogists.

State Papers: James I and Charles I also occasionally granted wine licences, and notes of these licences are given in the *Calendars of State Papers Domestic*. The names of only some of the licensees and the towns in which they lived are given in the calendars. More detailed information may be found in the original State Papers.

Declared Accounts of the Pipe Office: Wine Licences, 1614-24, 1670-1756 [E 351/ 3153-3197]. These are the accounts of annual rents, frequently paid in arrears, from wine retailers, received by the Receivers of Wine (the royal patentees) and later the Wine Commissioners, which were sent to the Exchequer. The accounts begin in 1566, but the early years are mostly in Latin and would appear to include few if any names. For most years 1614 to 1624 and from 1670 to 1756 long lists of licensees are recorded, together with the names of the towns in which they lived, but no inn signs.

The Wine Licence Office was established in 1679. Its accounts include names of defaulters and those in arrears, giving addressses, 1682-1757 [AO 3/1194-1242].

Ledgers of the Wine Duty Farmers [Guildhall Library, Manuscripts Dept., Mss. 15353-5]: From 1638 to about 1640 the Vintners' Company, London, were the Wine Receivers. Their accounts contains the names of a large number of London licensees, together with their inn or tavern signs and the names of the street and parish where located. A much smaller number of provincial licensees are listed.

County Quarter Sessions records: occasional references to licences to sell wine are found; **these have been noted when known**.

Borough records: some boroughs did issue wine licences during the sixteenth and seventeenth centuries. Records of these licences are usually not easy to find in the borough archives, and are rarely indexed. Note is given in this book only of those boroughs for which record of licences has been found.

The Universities of Cambridge and Oxford, the Borough of St. Albans and the Vintners Company of the City of London had special privileges for licensing taverns.

Spirit Seller and Spirit Licences, 1552 - 1828

Some counties granted licences to spirit retailers in the sixteenth, seventeenth and early eighteenth centuries, and records of these may be found in the Quarter Sessions rolls, files and order books.[5] However, these have rarely been catalogued by the record offices and **they are only occasionally noted in this Guide.**

The first law concerning spirits (spirituous liquors) was passed in 1690, but this was for encouraging distillation, and did not deal with the sale of spirits. By the early eighteenth century in London, if not elsewhere, spirits were being sold in taverns, inns, alehouses, brandy shops, dram shops and from cellars and street hawkers in great quantities. This is the period depicted by Hogarth and known as the gin era. Several Acts were passed, but it was not until 1751 that the sale of spirits was successfully brought under the control of the justices. By then spirit licences could only be issued to those already possessing an alehouse licence.

Spirit licences: very few were issued before 1751 and no provision appears to have been made for them to be registered or copies to be preserved.

---

5. Some licences were issued for some spirit retailers in the Tudor and early Stuart periods, and these may be found in the Quarter Sessions files, rolls and order books. *Buckinghamshire Sessional Rolls 1678-1694*, ed. William le Hardy (Bucks. Q.S. and C.C., 1933) contains examples, and also for licensed coffee sellers.

Constables' Returns of victuallers and sellers of spirits, licensed and unlicensed were ordered by the Middlesex magistrates in the 1720s, 1730s and 1740s.

Petty Sessions Minute Books: After 1751 these may contain records of unlicensed spirit retailers.

Full Publican Licences and Beer Licences, 1828 - today

The 1820s and 1830s mark a significant break in the history of licensing and the types of records kept. The 1828 Act repealed almost all the earlier licensing Acts and provided a new framework for granting licences to sell beer, wine, spirits and other excisable liquors, and for regulating inns and alehouses. Unfortunately, however, this Act made no provision for keeping records of the licences. Thus in most counties there are few licensing records for the four decades after this Act, except for the occasional applications for new licences and general orders etc which are sometimes found in the Quarter Sessions and Petty Sessions records.

After the 1828 Alehouses Acts many counties set up new Petty Sessional Divisions which were often also the Licensing Divisions.

In 1830 the Beerhouse Act, passed to encourage the sale of beer, brought into being beer retailers who kept beer shops, or beer houses; they could only sell beer and cider (as against public houses which could also sell wine and spirits). Licence for these could be obtained on demand from the local excise office; beer retailers did not have to acquire a licence at the annual Brewster Sessions. The regulations were amended in 1834 and 1840 by which date a property qualification was required for new beer retailers and parish officers had to provide certificates as to the rateable value of the premises. These Beerhouse Acts were repealed in 1869, from which date new beer house licences were issued by the justices. In 1872 the regulation and licensing of all beer shops came under the control of justices of the peace. Very few areas have licensing records relating to beer shops before 1872.

Duplicate overseers' rating certificates or other records show that the beer retailers occupied suitably rated property (1840 Beer Act).

There were now several types of licence – full publican's licence, the six day licence (full licence, but closed on Sundays), on- and off-beerhouse licences (that is licences for the sale of beer for consumption on and off the premises), and grocers' licences which allowed wine to be sold without the requirement of a magistrate's licence by shops and by refreshment houses (the wine to be drunk with food).

The Licensing Act of 1872 consolidated and tidied up the legislation and introduced a number of new features. It was once again mandatory to keep registers of licences granted annually at the Petty Sessions (Brewster Sessions). The licences were confirmed by a committee of justices appointed by Quarter Sessions.

Quarter Sessions records

County Licensing Committee records include minutes, annual reports, correspondence. The records also are concerned with general decisions of the committee, applications for licences and other business transferred from the Petty Sessions.

Licensing Returns. These are usually very detailed lists of the licensed premises giving details of licensee, inn sign, location, owner and leaseholder, and perhaps also the proximity of other licensed premises, date of first licence if granted since 1830 or 1869, type of customers etc.

Petty Sessions records
Minutes, reports, correspondence and papers of the licensing committees of individual
  Licensing Divisions.
Registers for the individual Licensing Divisions. There are several different kinds:
  Registers of Licences:
    1. Full publican licences renewed at brewster sessions;
    2. Beer retailer's licences renewed at brewster sessions
    (these usually give the names of licensees, inn signs and addresses);
  Registers of transfer of licences;
  Registers of applications for licences: these may deal with application for new
    licences or a change from beer-only to full licence. The decision of the court and
    other details may be included.
Court registers may include details of licences together with other court information.
Licensing maps and plans: these include maps showing the location of a public house
or beer shop and its proximity to other licensed premises, as well as detailed plans of
alterations to the premises. The latter may reflect the changing attitudes of the licensing
justices and the aspirations of the breweries to improve their public houses and beer
shops.

Twentieth century petty session licensing records which have not been deposited in
the county record office may have been retained by the present licensing court. It may
be possible to consult them there.

Until 1904 magistrates could refuse to renew a licence to houses against which no
complaint of misconduct had been made. The 1904 Compensation Act inaugurated a
system whereby owners of licensed premises and the licensees could be compensated
when a renewal was refused (unless because it was a disorderly house etc). This Act
resulted in much work for the county licensing committees and corresponding records.
The effect of later licensing Acts on licensed premises may also be found in the county
committee papers.

County records or Quarter Sessions records
  Compensation Authority Committee minute books, papers, correspondence, registers,
lists, petitions, financial statements, etc
  These are concerned with the workings of the 1904 Compensation Act and usually
give the names of public houses considered for closure, and may include reports,
valuations and plans.

Police records
  These include Chief Constable's reports and registers of licensed premises. They
have been included when these are listed with other licensing records by the record
office. Bridgeman and Emsley's *Guide to the Archives of the Police Forces of England
and Wales* (The Police History Society, 1989) includes references of a similar nature.
All police authorities still holding records relevant to this Guide have been circulated for
up-to-date information, and details of the small number that responded have been
shown as appropriate. In general archives still in police custody are difficult of access
with few if any full time archivists.

Newspapers
  Reports of the brewster sessions and the policies of the licensing magistrates may be
reported in the newspapers and may well provide information not found in other
surviving records. ***Details of these are not included in this Guide.***

Other Licences

Innkeepers and publicans were also required to obtain licences for other services offered to their customers.

Music and dancing: houses in London and Westminster used for dancing and other public entertainment required a licence under an Act of 1752. Licences were required for houses in the rest of the country from later in the century.

Post horses: Licences for the houses hiring out post horses were required by an Act of 1784.

Concluding Notes

Licensing records present several difficulties. In many counties records have not been listed in detail and without inspection it is not possible to know whether they contain records of licensees or licensed premises. This is particularly true of Quarter Sessions rolls and order books.

It has not been possible to be consistent in listing those Quarter Sessions records and researchers should consult published and typescript calendars and indexes where these are available.

Legislation did not always clearly lay down what records should be kept, and consequently there is a great diversity in types of records and the names by which they were known.

We have tried to list the documents **under the title** by which they are catalogued or known in the record office or library where they are held.

A very different kind of difficulty arises from the variety of establishments which are the predecessors, more or less, of our present public houses and inns. The most important ones for the early period dealt with in this Guide are inns, alehouses, and taverns. They were thought of as quite different types of houses and they or their keepers were separately listed in the Certificate of Inns, Taverns and Alehouses returned to the government in 1577.[6]

By the end of the eighteenth century terminology had changed and mid-nineteenth century directories frequently separate the houses into three different groups: inns and hotels; taverns and public houses; and beerhouses. See the Glossary (pages 61-63) for a list of the most common names for the various types of houses and their licensees.

As far as possible the licensing records for each county have been grouped in the order given in the introduction with the exception that nationally held records, mostly of wine and spirits licensing, have been placed at the start. Variations reflect the way in which records are catalogued by the different record offices or how the questionnaire was completed.

Only those records known, or thought to have licensing references, have been included. The information is taken from questionnaires completed by the staff of the record offices and libraries and from the compilers' own researches. All corrections, amendments and additions will be gratefully received.

Military Survey, 1756

This national survey [*TNA* WO.30/49] provides totals of lodging and stabling in various places and areas. Though not relating to licensing as such, occasionally names of licensees and their inns are given. These were for Cornwall (Bodmin), Hertfordshire, Suffolk (Framlingham and Saxmundham) and some west Welsh districts. Details are given under county entries. My thanks to Mrs Sue Lumas for checking this for me. **J.G.**

---

6. TNA, SP 12/119. The names of the 'licensees' are only given on the returns for Berkshire and Buckinghamshire.

Arrangement of the listings (by pre-1974 English and Welsh counties)

Boroughs which were their own licensing authorities; post-1828 Licensing Districts. Information included as provided, but clearly often incomplete or missing entirely.

National Records held at The National Archives and elsewhere *(chronologically)*

Letters Patent (1554-71) [The National Archives, *Calendars of State Papers Domestic*].
Vintners' Fines (1569-72) and Informations (1566-7, 1569/70, 1583-9) [T.N.A.. E176].
Victuallers' (Lenten) Recognizances (1572-1634) [T.N.A. E180, C203].
Wine licences (1583-1602) [T.N.A. C238]; (1626-39) [Worcestershire Record Office].
Sir Giles Mompesson's inn licences (1617-20) [T.N.A.; House of Lords Record Office; p'copy at the Centre for Buckinghamshire Studies, D/X 648]. Places named as in 1620.
Wine Licences: Pipe Office (1614-24, 1670-1756) [T.N.A. E351/3153-3197].
Ledgers of Wine Duty Farmers. Vintners' Company, 1638 40 (mainly London) [Guildhall Library, Department of Manuscripts, Mss. 15353-5].
Military Survey (1756). [T.N.A. WO30/49].

Records held in County and City Record Offices and Libraries

Note. It has been impractical to include documentary references for local authority records. However, most county repositories have been provided with a fully referenced version of their county section, which should be available there on request.

1552-1828: Inns and Alehouses
County Quarter Sessions records
Petty Sessions records
Borough and Town records
Family papers and Estate papers

1828 onwards: Inns, Public Houses and Beer Houses
Quarter Sessions records
Other County records
Petty Sessions records arranged in licensing districts
Any other records

Other Licences for any other beverage and music and dancing
Wine licences granted by Boroughs
Mompesson inn licences
Spirit licensing records
Music and dancing licences
Post Horse licences

Abbreviations

acs	accounts	memo	memorandum, memoranda
amal	amalgamated	mins	minutes, minute boks
cert	certificate	misc	miscellaneous
corres	correspondence	PH	Public House
ctee	committee	PS	Petty Sessions
Div	Division	QS	Quarter Sessions
exam	examination	re	relating to, concerning
incl	including	recogs	recognizances
JPs	Justices of the Peace	refs	references
lic(s)	licence(s), licensing	reg(s)	register(s)
lic'd	licensed	vol	volume

BEDFORDSHIRE

Boroughs which were their own licensing authority: Bedford, Luton.

Licensing Districts set up in 1829: Ampthill, Bletsoe (renamed Sharnbrook 1871), Bedford County, Bedford Borough, Biggleswade, Woburn (amalgamated with Leighton Buzzard 1953), Leighton Buzzard (created 1854), Luton (Luton Borough separate division from 1876), Dunstable (from 1864).

National records (see pages 6-8)

Letters Patent (1554-71): Dunstable.
Vintners' fines (1569-72): Dunstable.
Victuallers' (Lenten) Recognizances (1572-1634).
Raleigh Wine Licences (1582-5, 1593-4, 1595-6, 1600-1).
Mompesson Licences (1620): Ampthill, Eaton Socon, Elstow, Henslow, Leighton Buzzard, Milton Ernest, Potton, Shefford, Southill, Westoning.
Coventry Wine Licences (1626-39): Ampthill, Bedford, Biggleswade, Blunham, Caldicott, Dunstable, Hockliffe, Leighton Buzzard, Salford, Woburn.
Wine Licences: Pipe Office (1670-1756).

Bedfordshire & Luton Archives & Record Service, The Record Office, Bedford.

1552-1828: Inns and Alehouses

County Quarter Sessions records
Recognizances 1726-1793, for county and some for Bedford Borough, a few only, see QS index.
Victuallers' registers 1822-29, indexed by parish.

Borough records
Bedford Quarter Sessions minutes 1586-1605, 1649-51, 1771-1828.
Bedford alehouse recognizances 1752, 1759, 1761.

1828 on: Inns, Public Houses and Beer Shops

Quarter Sessions records
Sessions Rolls and Order Book, occasional references as a court of appeal for licences refused at Petty Sessions.

Other county records
County Licensing Committee mins 1873-1974; Compensation ledgers 1905-66; County licensing in-letter files 1905-21; County licensing out-letter books 1905-53; Licensing Committee papers and reports 1905-67.

Petty Sessions records
Minutes of Special Sessions, including alehouses: Biggleswade 1871-1903.
Minutes of Licensing Ctee: Sharnbrook 1913-37.

Bedfordshire & Luton Archives & Record Service continued

Petty Sessions continued
Alehouse licence registers: Ampthill 1872-1995 (minor gaps); Bedford District 1903-35, *c*1955-95; Bedford Borough 1890-1901, *c*1955-95; Biggleswade 1872-1915,1956-1995; Dunstable 1874-79,1887,1889, 1906-53 ; Leighton Buzzard *c*1860s-1956; Luton District 1872-1964; Luton Town (Borough from 1876) 1872-1876, 1929-54; Sharnbrook *c*.1901-30, *c*1955-95; Woburn 1868-1953; North Bedfordshire including Bedford Borough 1976-80.
N.B. Petty Sessions minute book and register entries can sometimes fill gaps in the above

Other records
Bedford Borough Police returns of fully licensed premises *c*.1890-1946 [photocopy].
Bedford Borough Police register of beer licences and for licensed houses *c*.1890-*c*.1946 [Microfiche 79].
Fire Service records include applications for PH lics and music and dancing records 1960s-80s [closed].

Other licences
Luton Borough, PS regs of music and dancing lics 1897-1931; see Fire Service records above.

BERKSHIRE

Boroughs which held their own Quarter Sessions: Abingdon, Maidenhead, Newbury, New Windsor, Reading, Wallingford, Wokingham.

Petty Sessional divisions: Abingdon borough, Abingdon county, Faringdon, Forest, Hungerford, Hungerford and Lambourn (formed 1964), Ilsley, Lambourn, Maidenhead borough, Maidenhead county, Moreton, Moreton and Wallingford (formed 1954), Newbury borough, Newbury county, Reading borough, Reading county (later Bradfield and Sonning), Wallingford borough, Wantage, Windsor borough, Windsor county.

National records (see pages 6-8)

Letters Patent (1554-71): Faringdon, Hungerford, Maidenhead, Newbury, Reading, New Windsor, Wantage.

Vintners' fines (1569-72): Abingdon, Charnham Street (was in Wiltshire), Reading, Wallingford.

Victuallers' (Lenten) Recognizances (1572-1634).

Raleigh Wine Licences (1582-7, 1588-9, 1593-5, 1596-7).

Mompesson Licences (1620): Abingdon, Blewbury, (Chipping) Faringdon, Longworth, Maidenhead, Pangbourne, Reading, Speenhamland, Sonning, Thatcham, Theale, Wallingford, Wantage, Windsor.

Coventry Wine Licences (1626-1639): Abingdon, Maidenhead, Reading, Speenhamland, Theale, Twyford, Wallingford, Wantage, Wokingham.

Wine Licences: Pipe Office (1670-1756).

Berkshire Record Office, *Reading.*

1552-1828: Inns and Alehouses

Quarter Sessions records
Original recognizances 1814-15, Forest, Ilsley, Maidenhead and Reading Divisions.

Borough and other town records
Abingdon: Lists of licensed victuallers with some original recogs; Annual bundles of recogs 1740-1839; Certificates of good character 1792-97.
Maidenhead: One alehouse recognizance 1763.
Newbury: Manorial Court Book 1640-1723 contains presentments of unlicensed houses.
Reading: Corporation diary contains some licensing records.
Wallingford: Borough minute book 1507-1683 contains victuallers recogs; Reg of alehouse lics 1784-1871.
New Windsor: Precedent Book of Oaths contains lists of lic'd and unlic'd inns and alehouses 1657, 1663; Sessions Books contain victuallers' regs 1720-1828; Sessions rolls for 1761 and 1768-9 contain some original recogs and certificates of good character for New Windsor only.
Wokingham: Sessions Book contains victuallers' registers 1777-1852.

Berkshire Record Office, continued

Estate records
Letter asking justices for a licence [D/EL1 C1/87].
Victuallers' register for the Hundreds of Ock and Horner in Abingdon Division 1765-76 [D/EP4/07].

1828 on: Inns, Public Houses and Beer Shops

County Quarter Sessions records
Minutes of the licensing committee 1905-73; Licensing papers 1903-62.

Borough and Town records
See left, 1552-1828.

Petty Sessions records
Note: with the exception of registers of alehouse licences, petty sessions records are closed for thirty years; records of the court in session include licensing information.
Registers of alehouse licences: Forest div c.1903-71; Ilsley div 1872-1901; Lambourn div 1872-1901; Maidenhead borough 1872-1962; Maidenhead county div 1872-1962; Moreton div 1872-1947; Reading borough 1869-1961; Reading county div 1875-1927; Wallingford borough 1872-1953; Wantage div 1892-1903; Windsor borough 1926-61; Windsor county div 1927-80.
Licensing maps and plans of licensed premises: Abingdon county div c.1912-24; Faringdon div c.1910-20; Forest div 1903-53; Lambourn div c.1913; Maidenhead borough 1911; Maidenhead county div. c.1910-1924; Moreton div c.1900-33; Moreton and Wallingford div 1954-69; Newbury borough 1913; Newbury county div c.1900-10; Reading county div c.1910-50; Wallingford borough c.1930s-1940s; Wantage div c.1930; Windsor borough c.1900-14; Windsor county div. 1907-60.
Licensing papers: Forest div 1880-1960; Maidenhead county div c.1883-1903; Moreton div 1932-55; Moreton and Wallingford div c.1950-70; Reading county div 1950-63; Wallingford borough 1934-47; Windsor county div 1931-33 .
Licensing reports by borough justices: Reading borough 1903-32.
Licensing compensation papers: Reading borough 1905-63.
Details of licensed houses in Caversham and Tilehurst 1913.
Minutes of licensing sessions and licensing committees: Reading borough 1883-1960.

Other licences
Premises licensed for music and dancing: Moreton division 1947-48; Reading borough 1926-64.

Thames Valley Police Museum, *Police Training College, Sulhampstead, Reading.*

Reading Borough Police
Register of public houses, 1896.
Chief Constable's reports to the licensing committee, 4 vols., 1898-1946.

BUCKINGHAMSHIRE

Boroughs which were their own licensing authority:
Buckingham, High Wycombe.
Licensing Districts post-1828 (not complete):
Aylesbury Borough, Amersham, Brill, Buckingham
(county), Buckingham Borough, Burnham,
Chesham, Marlow, Stoke, Winslow, Wycombe
(county), Wycombe Borough.

National records (see pages 6-8)

Letters Patent (1554-71): Colnbrook, Eton, Great
Missenden, Newport Pagnell.
Vintners' fines (1569-72): Britwell, Buckingham.
Victuallers' Recognizances (1572-1634): None.
Raleigh Wine Licences (1582-7, 1593-4, 1595-6).
Mompesson Licences (1620) (see under 'Family
Papers', below): Aylesbury, Bottle Claydon(?),
Brill, Burnham, Chesham, Long Crendon, Eton,
Fenny Stratford, Great Marlow, Marsh Gibbon,
Olney, Princes Risborough, Slough (Upton), Stony
Strat-ford, Wendover, West Wickham, Weston
Turville.
Coventry Wine Licences (1626-1639): Beaconsfield,
Buckingham, Chalfont, Chesham, Colnbrook, Eton,
Farnham Royal, Ivinghoe, Little Marlow, Missenden,
Slough, Wendover, Wooburn.
Wine Licences: Pipe Office (1670-1756).
Military Survey 1756 (see page 11). Beaconsfield,
see entry under Hertfordshire.].

Centre for Buckinghamshire Studies, Aylesbury.

1552-1828: Inns and Alehouses

Quarter Sessions records
Sessions Rolls, from 1700, numerous early
references; Sessions Order Books, from 1678;
Recognizances, some Hundreds only, 1763-1791;
Victuallers' Registers 1753-1828. Those for
Burnham and Stoke Hundreds, 1753, published in
Heritage (Windsor, Slough & Dist FHS, **7**.1,
Autumn 1978).

Buckingham Borough Records
Victuallers' Registers 1790-1828.

Petty Sessions Records
Original licences, Aylesbury 1797.

Family papers
Sir Giles Mompesson Account Books, 1617-1620
[photocopy D/X 648] (see above and page 6).
Mompesson lic.: one only for Olney 1618 [D/B 85].
Diary of Sir Roger Hill, JP 1689-1705 (gaps) lists lics
granted, Stoke Petty Sessions [D/W/97 8].

1828 on: Inns, Public Houses and Beer Shops

County Licensing Committee records
Licensing maps and plans: A few plans only,
prepared for Bucks. Licensing Ctee, 20th century.
Licensing Returns, for whole county, 1872.
Minutes 1904-73 [Q/CM/4/1-5].

Centre for Buckinghamshire Studies continued

Petty Session Records
Papers of the clerk to the Aylesbury petty sessions
justices, includes applications for alehouse and
beerhouse licences, licensing hours, memorandum, and lists of houses 1834-41.
Petty Sessions continued
Alehouse Registers: Amersham c.1935-67; Brill
1881-1902; Buckingham (county) 1872-1902;
Buckingham Borough 1872-84 ; Burnham 1935-
1956, 1957-71; Chesham 1872-1903; Marlow
1897-1902, 1911-70; Winslow 1908-1929;
Wycombe (county) 1879-1954, 1866-1895, 1954-
1974; Wycombe Borough c.1909-53.

Other licences

County Quarter Session records
Occasional refs to coffee house and spirit licences.

High Wycombe Library.

Chipping Wycombe Quarter Sessions records
Robert Peck's notebook, town clerk 1717-54,
includes notes on licensing issues.

CAMBRIDGESHIRE

Boroughs which were their own licensing authority:
Cambridge University had jurisdiction over the
town of Cambridge and parish of Chesterton for
licensing purposes up to 1856;
Wisbech.

National records (see pages 6-8)

Letters Patent (1554-71): Cambridge, Caxton.
Vintners' fines (1569-72): None.
Victuallers' (Lenten) Recognizances (1572-1634).
*Raleigh Wine Licences (1582-3, 1584-7, 1593-4,
1596-7).*
Mompesson Licences (1620): Balsham, Brinkley,
Cambridge, Caxton, Dullingham, Ely (Isle of),
Fordham, Islein(?), Kneesworth, Newton,
Witchford, (Gt.) Wilbraham, Wisbech, West
Wratting.
Coventry Wine Licences (1626-1639): Bottisham,
Fowlmere, Linton, Soham, Wisbech.
Wine Licences: Pipe Office (1670-1756).

Cambridge University Library

See D.M. Owen, *Cambridge University Archives: A
Classified List*, under 'Vintners' etc, 1557-1913.

Victuallers' registers for Cambridge and parish of
Chesterton 1552, 1606-1856 (m'film at C.R.O.).
Isle of Ely licensed victuallers recognizances 1613,
1622, 1624, 1627, 1653-54, 1656-57, 1660-64,
1755-75.

Cambridgeshire continued

Cambridgeshire Archives, *Cambridge.*

1552-1828: Inns and Alehouses

Cambridge University records
Victuallers' registers for Cambridge and parish of
Chesterton 1552, 1606-1856, microfilm [original
regs are held by Cambridge University Library].

Quarter Sessions records
Volumes of recognizances of Cambridgeshire
county victuallers 1728-58, 1764-1828.
Isle of Ely licensed victuallers' recognizances
register 1822-23.
Note. Most Isle of Ely Quarter Sessions records
prior to 1836 are in *Cambridge University Library.*

Petty Sessions records
Ely and South Witchford Petty Sessions Division:
Ale-house minutes granted 1740-1918 (regs of
alehouse certificates).
See also below under 'Minutes and court registers'.

1828 on: Inns, Public Houses and Beer Shops

Petty Sessions records
Registers of licences: Arrington and Melbourn Petty
Sessions Div 1939-68; Bottisham PS Div. 1903-
1968; Cambridge Borough (later City)1872-1946;
Cambridge PS Div 1923-68; Caxton PS Div 1943-
1968; Ely and South Witchford Div: Alehouse mins
- see above, Alehouse regs 1875-88, 1901-1911,
Beerhouse mins (regs of certs granted) 1869-
1918, Beerhouse regs 1875-88, 1901-11, Lic regs
(alehouse, beer) 1912-70; Linton PS Div 1949-68;
Newmarket PS Div 1875-92, 1898-1968; North
Witchford PS Div: Chatteris subdiv 1872-1927,
1929-69; March subdiv 1921-69; Whittlesey PS
Div 1927-69; Wisbech Borough PS Div 1872-99,
1906-69; Wisbech PS Div 1925-1969.
Minute books and court registers (not all of these
have been checked, but some do record transfers,
applications etc): Arrington and Melbourn, court
regs 1913-80, mins 1946-57; Bottisham, court regs
1880-1980, mins 1876-81; Cambridge Borough,
court regs 1869-1983, mins 1878-1959;
Cambridge PS Div, court regs 1863-1875, 1903-
1977, incl recogs of lics from 1863, mins 1895-
1957; Caxton, court regs 1934-80, mins 1945-57;
Ely and South Witchford, court regs 1880-1983,
mins 1796-1806, 1872-1977, lic min 1879-95;
Linton, court reg 1915-80, mins 1873-1957;
Newmarket, court regs 1880-1983, mins 1880-
1940, lic mins 1903; North Witchford PS Div lic
mins 1842-69; North Witchford, March subdiv
court regs 1915-70, mins 1935-76; North
Witchford, Chatteris subdiv court regs 1915-68,
mins 1899-1976; Whittlesey, court regs 1915-70,
mins 1895-1976; Wisbech Borough, court regs
1915-70; Wisbech, court regs 1946-70, mins 1944-
1960.
Register of convictions for licensing offences: Ely
and South Witchford PS Div 1867-1902.

Cambridgeshire Archives continued

Petty Sessions continued
Licensing returns: Arrington and Melbourn Div 1903;
Cambridge Div, list 1882; Isle of Ely return 1906;
Linton Div, list of licensed houses 1903.
Licensing maps - a few.

Police records
Chief Police Officer's annual reports to lic JPs 1892-
1945 (incomplete), Ely and South Witchford Div.
Licensing registers for Arrington and Melbourn,
Bottisham, Cambridge (county, not Borough),
Caxton, Lindon and Newmarket PS Divisions 1945-
1970.

Other licences
Music and dancing licences: Newmarket PS Div
1953-73; North Witchford, Chatteris subdiv 1950-
1965; North Witchford, March subdiv 1950-69.

Note. No relevant records are held by the *Wisbech
and Fenland Museum.*

CHESHIRE

Boroughs which were their own licensing authority:
Chester.

National records (see pages 6-8)

Letters Patent (1554-71): Chester, Nantwich, West
Chester.
Vintners' fines (1569-72): Chester, Congleton,
Northwich, West Kirby.
Alehouse Recognizances (1580-1640): Palatinate.
Raleigh Wine Licences (1582-3).
Mompesson Licences (1620): None.
Coventry Wine Licences (1626-1639): Brereton,
Chester, Frodsham, Church Hulme, Knutsford,
Malpas, Northwich, Winnington.
Wine Licences: Pipe Office (1670-1756).

Cheshire and Chester Archives and Local Studies, Chester.

1552-1828: Inns and Alehouses
Quarter Sessions records
Alehouse keepers' regs 1743-58, 1827-28.
Recognizances 1629-41, 1749-1828.

Chester City Quarter Sessions: Vols of victuallers'
recognizances 1552-1688 (gaps); QS file 1594-
1595 contains lists of persons selling ale and beer
about 1550; files may also contain present-ments
etc; vols of victuallers' recogs 1736-1825.
Other Borough records: Mayor's Books contain
some recogs 1561/62 on.

Cheshire continued

1828 on: Inns, Public Houses and Beer Shops

Petty Sessions records
Records, including in many cases registers of alehouses, licensed victuallers, premises licensed for music and dancing, and billards, are held for the following petty sessions divisions:
Broxton 1835-1974; Bucklow 1859-53; Chester Castle 1890-1977; Congleton (formerly SE Ches) 1967-81; Congleton Borough 1891-1967; Congleton County 1880-1967; Crewe Borough 1880-1957; Daresbury 1872-1973; Dukinfield 1859-1957; Eddisbury 1848-1958; Ellesmere Port Borough 1916-52; Ellesmere Port and Nelson 1979-83; Hyde 1837-1907; Macclesfield Borough 1915-51; Middlewich 1910-67; Nantwich 1886-1952; Prestbury 1881-1949; Runcorn 1896-1968; Sandbach 1920-71; Warrington Borough 1880-1975; Warrington County 1863-1974; Widnes 1892-1970; Wirral 1872-1967.

Chester Borough Quarter Sessions records: Reg of licensed alehouse keepers 1829-33.

Chester Petty Sessions records: Regs of lics (various types) c.1872-1970; Mins of lic sessions 1864-1942; Magistrates lic papers re PHs etc 1895-1974.

Licences for other activities

Chester Borough records: Assembly book, records names of vintners licensed to sell wine, 1567; letter re enforcement of regulations re vintners' lics 1605.

Petty Sessions records: Regs of music and dancing licences c.1921-70 .

Stockport Magistrates' Court records
Stockport County: five regs of public house, beer house, beer off, wine and spirit off, sweets, billiards licences 1892-1928; reg of publicans, clubs, restaurants, beer, wines and spirits, beer, wine and spirits off, music, singing and dancing, cinemas and supper licences 1956-74.
Stockport Borough: Magistrates' Order Book, two regs of lics to be renewed 1878-1906; General Annual Lic Meetings and Special Sessions mins 1918-41; General Annual Lic Meeting and Transferring Lic Sessions mins 1949-73; eight regs of publicans' lics (some incl. off-licences) 1872-1954; three regs of off-licences 1903-54; reg of beerhouse lics 1912-74; reg of off-licences 1955-74; reg of publicans' lics 1955-74; reg of licensing Transfer Sessions 1976-82.

Other licences
Stockport Borough: four regs of music and dancing lics 1891-1974; reg of billiard lics 1912-74.
Stockport Combined: reg of music, singing and dancing lics 1980-81.

Petty Sessions records: Dukinfield PS Div (covering townships of Dukinfield, Godley, Hollingworth, Hyde, Matley, Newton, Tintwistle, Werneth): Regs of lics, all types, 1886-7.

Birkenhead Sessions records
Lic Ctee mins, 3 vols 1905-59; reports of visits of inspection 1931; Lic Planning ctee mins, 2 vols, 1949-57; Birkenhead Compensation Authority mins, 1905-1938; Compensation Fund acs 1905-1974; reg of lics referred, reasons for refusals to renew 1906-27; regs of lics, 17 vols, contain considerable details about each, 1880-1952. Regs of lic transfers, 4 vols, 1910-63.

Wallasey Sessions records
Regs of lics, 8 vols, 1916-61.

CORNWALL

Letters Patent (1554-71): Bodmin, Launceston, St. Goran, Truro.
Vintners' fines (1569-72): Bodmin, East Looe, Fowey, Grampound, Goran, Gwendron, Gwinear, Helston, Kellington, Launceston, Looe, Manaccan, Margham, Market Jew, Mawgan, Megavissey, Mitchell, Newland, Newport, Padstow, Penryn, Penzance, Polruan, Probus, Redruth, St. Agnes, St. Austell, St. Columb, St. Ives, St. Just in Roseland, St. Keverne, Saltash, Stratton, Tregony, Tewoon, Truro.
Victuallers' Recognizances (1572-1634): None.
Raleigh Wine Licences (1582-4).
Mompesson Licences (1620): Liskeard, Saltash, Truro.
Coventry Wine Licences (1626-1639): Crasthole[?], Egloshayle, Fowey, Helston, Milbrook in Maker, Padstow, St Columb Major, Tregoney.
Wine Licences: Pipe Office (1670-1756).
Military Survey 1756 (see page 11). Bodmin District: places, names of victuallers and signs, numbers of beds and stabling [WO 30/49, ff.26-27].

No licensing records known to survive.

CUMBERLAND

Boroughs which were their own licensing authority:
Carlisle.

> **National records** (see pages 6-8)

Letters Patent (1554-71): None.
Vintners' fines (1569-72): Carlisle.
Victuallers' Recognizances (1572-1634): None.
Raleigh Wine Licences (1582-7).
Mompesson Licences (1620): None.
Coventry Wine Licences (1626-1639): 'Greby'[?],
Whitehaven.
Wine Licences: Pipe Office (1670-1756).

> **Cumbria Record Office,** *Carlisle.*

1552-1828: Inns and Alehouses

Quarter Sessions records
Session rolls, 1688-1700 contain only six references
to licensing; Original recogs, one only, for 1788;
Alehouse recog regs 1753-72; Alehouse regs
1822-31; Legal opinion re licensing, 1739; Affidavit
re alehouse licensing 1788.
Carlisle Borough records: Forms for alehouse lics,
two, 1681, 1687; reg of publicans and public
houses licensed 1822-32.

1828 on: Inns, Public Houses and Beer Shops

Quarter Sessions records
Licensing returns, Eskdale Ward of the county,
1892; County lic ctee 1872-1918; Returns of
licensed houses 1915, 1932.

Carlisle Borough records: Regs of premises
licensed to sell liquor 1872-1899.

Petty Sessions
Alston Div 1909-84 (out-store, 48 hours notice).
Brampton: regs of premises licensed to sell liquor
1947-71.
Cumberland Ward: regs of alehouse lics 1840-1904.
Keswick: regs of lic'd premises 1889-1967.
Leath ward: reg of alehouse lics 1872-73.
Longtown: regs of alehouse lics 1872-1910.

Constabulary records (also at out-store)
Carlisle and County licensing division (not city)
1901-1963.
Penrith and Alson licensing diition 1890-1972.
Keswick: register of licensed premises 1900-73.

> **Cumbria Record Office & LS Library,** *Whitehaven.*

Petty Sessions
Cockermouth: regs of alehouse lics 1856-1934;
lists of lic'd houses 1904-23; Police reports on
licensing 1932-46; plans of proposed alterations to
alehouses 1904-66.
Workington: reg of liquor lics 1911-57.

> **Cumbria Record Office & LS Library,** *Whitehaven.*

Petty Sessions records, regs of lics:
Penrith Div 1927-48.

DERBYSHIRE

Boroughs which were their own licensing authority:
Derby
Licensing Districts post-1828:
Alfreton, Appletree, Ashbourne, Belper, Buxton,
Derby Borough, Derby County, Ilkston, Long
Eaton, Matlock, Repton, Ripley, Swadlincote, and
Wirksworth.

> **National records** (see pages 6-8)

Letters Patent (1554-71): Derby.
Vintners' fines (1569-72): Chesterfield, Derby.
Victuallers' (Lenten) Recognizances (1572-1634).
Raleigh Wine Licences (1582-7, 1596-7).
Mompesson Licences (1620): None.
Coventry Wine Licences (1626-1639): Buxton,
Chapel en le Frith, Derby, Sudbury.
Wine Licences: Pipe Office (1670-1756).

> **Derbyshire Record Office,** *Matlock.*

1552-1828: Inns and Alehouses

Quarter Sessions records
Registers of victuallers' recognizances 1753-1827.

1828 on: Inns, Public Houses and Beer Shops

Petty Sessions
Regs of licences: Alfreton 1924-59; Appletree 1890-
1954; Ashbourne 1903-58; Bakewell 1872-1968;
Belper 1872-1901; Buxton 1887-1971; Chapel-en-
le-Frith (High Peak) 1872-1969; Derby Borough
1877-1978; Derby County 1927-55; Glossop
1897-1969; Ilkeston 1962-1968; Long Eaton
1953-68; Matlock 1906-55; Repton 1927-1955;
Regs of Lics: Ripley and Heanor 1961-67;
Swadlincote 1887-1971; Wirksworth 1879-1900.
Minutes of annual licensing sessions: Alfreton and
Clay Cross 1868-1938; Appletree 1883-1967;
Bakewell 1857-1976; Wirksworth 1868-1884.
Brewster returns and files on licence application:
Alfreton and Clay Cross 1944-49.

Inherited records: Derby Borough
Compensation Authority: Mins 1905-74; Financial
statements 1905-14; Lics extinguished 1905-07;
Ledgers 1905-60.

Other licences
Music and dancing licences: Alfreton 1961-76;
Buxton 1881-1975; Belper 1948-77; Chapel-en-le-
Frith 1965-75; Derby Borough 1893-1978;
Glossop 1908-1975.

> **Derby Central Library,** *Derby.*

Derby Borough records: Largely unlisted.

DEVON

Boroughs which were their own licensing authority:
Barnstaple, Bideford, Exeter, Okehampton,
Plymouth, Plympton, South Molton, Torrington,
Totnes.

Licensing Divisions post-1828:
Barnstaple, Bideford, Bradninch, Dartmouth,
Devonport, Exeter, Okehampton, Plymouth,
Plympton, South Molton, Tavistock, Tiverton,
Torquay, Great Torrington, and Totnes.

National records (see pages 6-8)

Letters Patent (1554-71): Barnstaple, Exeter,
Honiton, Kirton(?).
Vintners' fines (1569-72): Axminster, Bampton,
Barnstaple, Chaigley, Colyton, Crediton, Dart-
mouth, Exeter, Honiton, Kenton, Kingsbridge,
Ilfracombe, Moreleigh, New Bushel, Okehampton,
Plymouth, Plympton, South Molton, Tavistock,
Tiverton, Topsham, Totnes, Winkleigh,
Witheridge.
Victuallers' (Lenten) Recognizances (1572-1634).
Raleigh Wine Licences (1583-7, 1588-96).
Mompesson Licences (1620): East Budleigh,
Churchstanton, Colyton, Crediton, Culmstock,
Dunsford, Exeter, Exmouth, Honiton, (South)
Molton, Moretonhampstead, Newton, Newton
Abbott, Otterton, Ottery St. Mary, Plymouth,
Plympton, Tavistock, Tiverton, Topsham, Totnes,
Uffculme, Upottery, Willminton(?).
Coventry Wine Licences (1626-1639): Ashburton,
Axminster, Barnstaple, Colyton, Creston in
Plymstock, Cullompton, Exeter, Honiton, Milbrook
in Maker, Modbury, Okehampton, Ottery St Mery,
Plymouth, Plympton Earl, Sampford Peverell,
Tavistock, Totnes.
Wine Licences: Pipe Office (1670-1756).

Devon Record Office, *Exeter.*

1552-1828: Inns and Alehouses

Quarter Sessions records
Sessions files and order books include some
general orders relating to alehouses; returns of
recogs 1607-1735, indexed by parish; returns of
recogs by Div's *c.*1661-1828 (also include
licences for inns now in Plymouth (Plympton and
Plymstock), and other closeby areas); original
recogs 1754-1828, indexed by parish; victuallers'
regs 1753-84; victuallers' regs 1822-28.

Borough records
Exeter: recogs of ale sellers 1647; original recogs
1758-99.
Okehampton: original recogs 1624 and 1713-77 +
strays for 1839 and 1849.

1828 on: Inns, Public Houses and Beer Shops
Quarter Sessions records: Licensing return, printed
schedule of all licences in county 1903.
Exeter Borough records: Victuallers' reg 1874-1920
(48 hours notice required).

Other licences
Exeter Borough records: Wine licences 1553.

North Devon Record Office, *Barnstaple.*

1552-1828: Inns and Alehouses
Borough records
Barnstaple: Alehouse recogs 1591; victuallers'
recogs 1674-5, 1677, 1746-52, 1803-22.
South Molton: Alehouse recogs 1753-79.

1828 on: Inns, Public Houses and Beer Shops
Borough or Petty Session records
Regs, applications for lics: Barnstaple 1837-1947.
Registers of licences: Barnstaple 1872-1963;
Bideford Borough 1903-63; Bideford PS Div 1916-
1953; Braunton PS Div 1872-1962; Great
Torrington Borough 1933-54; Great Torrington PS
Div 1903-61; Holsworthy 1934-61; South Molton
Borough 1906-54; South Molton PS Div 1901-62.

Other licences
Music and dancing licences: Bideford Borough
1940-54.

Plymouth & West Devon Record Office.

1552-1828: Inns and Alehouses
Plymouth Borough records: Quarter Sessions Order
Books 1675-94, 1703-1808, include presentments
etc; lists of alehouse keepers in Vintry Ward 1661;
Petty Sessions 1703-1816, contents as above; Ale
and beer wayts 1617-32; Returns of number of
victualling houses in the Borough 1802-05, 1821-
1824; Victuallers and victualling houses 1802-29;
List of excise offenders 1804-05; Return of short
weights and measures 1822; Black Book 1534-
1730, White Book 1561-1754, contain general
statements and orders re licensing.

Other licences
Late 16th century draft indenture of wine dues;
some music and dancing lics are recorded in
Plymouth Corporation minutes.

1828 on: Inns, Public Houses and Beer Shops
Licensing committee minutes 1925-62.
Compensation Authority minutes 1905-74.

Devon & Cornwall Constabulary Museum, *Police HQ, Middlemoor, Exeter EX2 7HQ. Museum located on Marsh Barton Trading Estate. Prior appointment essential.*

Devon Constabulary
List of public houses in Exeter, 1800s.
Register of public houses in Plymouth, *c.*1930.

DORSET

National records (see pages 6-8)

Letters Patent (1554-71): Blandford Forum, Sherborne, Wimborne Minster.
Vintners' fines (1569-72): Beer, Blandford Forum, Bridport, Cerne, Dorchester, Evershot, Lyme Regis, Melcombe Regis, Milton, Poole, Puddletown, Shaftesbury, Sherborne, Tolpuddle, Wareham, Weymouth, Wimborne Minster.
Victuallers' (Lenten) Recognizances (1572-1634).
Raleigh Wine Licences (1582-7, 1593-7).
Mompesson Licences (1620): Beaminster, Bridport, Broadway, Broadwinsor, Chideock, Dorchester, Fordington, Frampton, Hawkchurch, Maiden Newton, Middle Marsh[?], South Perrott, Powerstock, Shaston (Shaftesbury?), Stalbridge, Stourton Caundle, Winterbourne Abbas.
Coventry Wine Licences (1626-39): Bridport, Chideock, Corfe Castle, Dorchester, Evershot, Gussage and Bere Regis, Lyme Regis, Puddletown, Weymouth and Melcombe Regis, Wimborne Minster.
Wine Licences: Pipe Office (1670-1756).

Dorset History Centre, *Dorchester.*

1552-1828: Inns and Alehouses

Quarter Sessions records
Regs of recogs (alehouses and victuallers] 38 vols, divisions of Dorchester, Cerne Abbas, Sherborne, Blandford Forum, Bridport, Shaftesbury, Sturminster Newton, 1714/15-1770. Names of inns from 1753.
Recogs, six bundles, 1754-1779, 1821.
Main series of Quarter Sessions rolls, dating from 1709, may contain information on licensing.

Borough records
Dorchester: Alehouse recog reg 1795-1828 ; Quarter Sessions rolls 1689-1831, some contain recogs.
Bridport: Alehouse keepers' bonds, 72 documents, 1581-1604; Lists of tipplers (alehouse keepers), drayers and brewers, 12 doc. 1591-1594; Vics' bonds for observance of Lent, 1609, 1615, eight documents;
Lyme Regis: Cert concerning inns, taverns and tippling houses 1596; Cert of innkeepers keeping disorderly houses 1790; Alehouse recogs 1605, 1613, 1614, 1625, 1694/5-1709, 1718, 1735-1780, 1784-1827; Alehouse lics 1687, 1796; Lists of alehouse lics 1723, 1724; Notices re lics.

1828 on: Inns, Public Houses and Beer Shops

Quarter Sessions records:
County Lic Ctee mins, 3 vols, 1872-1928; file of regulations under the 1902 Act and description of persons declared habitual drunkards.

Lyme Regis Borough records:
Lists of beer retailers 1830-34.

Poole Borough records:
Alehouse recognizances 1786-1830.
Other alehouse records 1620-1872 (205).

Co. DURHAM

Boroughs which were their own licensing authority: Durham.
Licensing Districts, post-1828: Durham Ward; Chester Ward - E, W, Middle and Gateshead Divisions; Darlington Ward - NW, SE and Stanhope Divs; Easington Ward - N, S, Seaham Harbour and Sunderland Divs; Stockton Ward - NE and SW Divs; Hartlepool Ward.
Post-1905: Barnard Castle and Staindrop Div, Bishop Auckland Div, Castle Eden Div, Chester-le-Street Div, Darlington Div, Durham Div Gateshead Div, Houghton-le-Spring Div, Lanchester, Consett and Stanley Div, Seaham Harbour Div, South Shields Div, Stanhope Div, Stockton Div, Sunderland Div, West Hartlepool Div, Wolsingham Div.

National records (see pages 6-8)

Letters Patent (1554-71): None.
Vintners' fines (1569-72): Darlington, Durham, Crossgate in Durham.
Alehouse Recognizances (1583-84): Palatinate.
Raleigh Wine Licences (1582-7, 1594-6).
Mompesson Licences (1620): None.
Coventry Wine Licences (1626-39): Chester le Street, Durham, Monkwearmouth, South Shields.
Wine Licences: Pipe Office (1670-1756).

Durham County Record Office, *Durham.*

1552-1828: Inns and Alehouses
Quarter Sessions
Sessions Order Books, 1616-1700, contain occasional details of recogs, orders and presentments; reg of victuallers' recogs 1716-18; constables' returns of alehouse keepers, and some certs of good character 1783-86, Chester, Stockton and Easington Wards; reg of recogs, Chester Ward 1804.

1828 on: Inns, Public Houses and Beer Shops

Quarter Sessions records
Lic ctee mins 1872-1938; plan of petty sessional divs under the 1904 Licensing Act August 1905.

Petty Sessions records
Bishop Auckland Division, lic regs: Darlington Ward NW, 1908-36; Barnard Castle 1935-74; Bishop Auckland 1937-66; Greta Bridge 1915-74; Stanhope 1896-1974; Wolsingham 1898-1974.
Castle Eden Division lic regs: Easington Ward South 1872-1961.
Chester-le Street Division: special sessions mins 1898-1953; declarations of JPs for holding special sessions 1884-1953; rough notebooks kept by JPs, 1884-1953; regs of applications 1966-73; lic regs 1885-1965, Chester Ward Middle; lists of PH lics, 1913.
Darlington Division: Lic reg 1930-66.

Co. Durham: *County R.O, Petty Sessions* contd.

Darlington Borough: Lic ctee mins 1915-46; regs of lics in SE Division 1872-81, 1883-1902, 1903-13; regs of lics in Darlington Borough 1903-12, 1914-1961; reg of lics transferred from Darlington 1972.

Durham City Division: eight lic regs, 1872-1930.

Durham County Division: lic regs 1901-15, 1916-56, Durham Ward.

Lanchester, Consett and Stanley Division: court lic reg 1957-66; Court reg of general annual lic meeting for West Div of Chester Ward, 1950-54; lic reg in the same div, 1901-56 ; list of lics, same div 1956; applications for transfer of lics, incl. plans, of three licensed premises 1954.

Borough records

Durham City: Records of convictions against licensed victuallers and beer retailers 1874-1907; Minutes of Brewster Sessions 1886-1906; particulars of offences 1885-1906.

Durham Brewster Session papers 1903-7. Details of licensed houses (c.1903-7).

South Shields: licensing minutes 1906-08.

Sunderland County: registers of clubs 1919-58.

Records transferred from Darlington Branch

Notices of applicants to sell liquor, 1833, 1887.

Notices of applicants to transfer licences 1887-8.

Durham Police records

These may contain records concerning licensing.

Licences for other activities

Music and dancing, theatre and billiards licence registers: Barnard Castle 1961-71; Greta Bridge 1956-71; Darlington Borough 1924-65; Durham County 1924-52, 1960-71; West Division Chester Ward 1911-54, 1955-76; Lanchester, Consett and Stanley 1955-66.

Teesside Archives, Middlesbrough.

Petty Session records

Hartlepool Borough: Alehouse licences 1853-7, 1859-60; Licensing registers 1872-1940.

West Hartlepool: Licensing registers 1903-62.

Tyne and Wear Archive Service, Newcastle upon Tyne.

Petty Sessions records

Blaydon: Beer, wine and spirit lic regs 1900-63.

Chester-le-Street (Washington Court): regs of lics to sell alcohol 1872-1960.

Gateshead: Alehouse/beerhouse regs 1879-1955.

Houghton-le-Spring PS Div of Easington Ward: lic (alehouse etc) regs 1903-76.

Jarrow Div of Durham County PS: lic reg for alehouses, beer, wine and spirits (on + off) lics 1903-55.

South Shields County and Hebburn PS Div: lic regs for alehouses etc 1912-60.

Police records

South Shields Borough Constabulary: Reg of public houses 1867-1902, 1931-52.

Tyne and Wear Archive Service continued

Other licences

Music and dancing licences: Blaydon 1923-53; Chester-le-Street 1925-53; Gateshead 1893-1955; Jarrow 1903-55; South Shields 1912-60.

ESSEX

Boroughs known to be their own licensing authority: Maldon.

Licensing Petty Sessions Divisions, post-1828: Becontree, Billericay (renamed Basildon 1990), Brentwood, Chelmsford, Colchester Borough, Dunmow, Dengie, Epping (amalgamated 1968), Epping and Ongar (formed 1968), Freshwell (amal. 1955), Freshwell and South Hinkford (formed 1955), South Hinkford, Braintree bench (amal. 1955), South Hinkford, Halstead bench (later Halstead div), Harwich borough, North Hinkford, Liberty of Havering-atte-Bower (abol. 1892), Harlow, Lexden and Winstree, Maldon borough, Ongar (amal. 1968), Orsett, Rochford, Redbridge, Romford (formed 1893, re-named Havering 1968), Saffron Walden borough (amal. 1959), Saffron Walden (formed 1959), Tendring, Walden (amal. 1959), Waltham Abbey (formed 1952, amal. 1966), Witham.

National records (see pages 6-8)

Letters Patent (1554-71): Aveley, Barking, Brentwood, Chelmsford, Colchester, Hornchurch, Kelvedon, Leigh, Maldon, Ratcliffe (?), Rayleigh, Romford, Thaxted.

Vintners' fines (1569-72): Barking, Bishops Stortford, Braintree, Brentwood, Coggeshall, Colchester, Chelmsford, Dunmow, Harwich, Hatfield Broad Oak, Ilford, Ingatestone, Kelvedon, Leigh, Pritwell, Romford, Saffron Walden, Thaxted, Waltham Abbey, West Ham.

Victuallers' (Lenten) Recognizances (1572-1634).

Raleigh Wine Licences (1582-7, 1589-90).

Mompesson Licences (1620): Abridge(?), Aldham, Ardleigh, Great Baddow, Great Bardfield, Blackmoore, Bradfield, Brentwood, Brook Street (South Weald), Chelmsford, Chigwell, (Chipping) Ongar, Colchester, Danbury, Great Dunmow, Epping, Fryerning, Gosfield, Harlow, Hempstead, Great Horkesley, Latton, Gt Oakley, Skipping Street (?), Steeple Bumpstead, Terling, Thorneton(?), Tillingham, Toppesfield, South Weald, Willingale Doe.

Coventry Wine Licences (1626-39): Bardfield, Barking, Blackmore, Braintree, Chadwellward, Chelmsford, Chigwell, Chipping Ongar, Colchester, Dagenham, Erith, Gosfield, Halstead, West Ham, Harestreet, Harwich, Horndon, Kelvedon, Orsett, Rainham, Rayleigh, Ripley Ward, Rochford, Romford, Saffron Walden, Stratford Langthorne, Upminster, Much Wakering, Walthamstow Toney, Witham, Wivenhoe, Woodford.

Wine Licences: Pipe Office (1670-1756).

Essex continued

1552-1828: Inns and Alehouses

Quarter Sessions records
Sessional Rolls 1556-1690, original recogs, petitions, indictments etc; Sessional Order Books 1652-1725, orders for suppression, resolution re alehouses 1625 etc; Presentment of alehouses 1644, 61 parishes; Original recogs 1580-1633, 1640; Victuallers' regs 1733, 1759-70,1769-1828. Rochford Hundred recognizances, 1769-1828.

Petty Sessions records
Epping Div JPs' exam and memo book incl. lists of licences for inns and alehouses, 1789-1794.
Liberty of Havering-atte-Bower Minute Book incl. lists of victuallers 1770-1832.

Maldon Borough records
View of Gannockers (alehouse keepers) 1557-1768; Precept to summon alehouse keepers 1635/6; Letter to Town Clerk as to alehouses, 17th cent.; Lics to keep alehouses 1624; Recog for not keeping victualling house 1620; Letter to Town Clerk re alehouses, 17th cent.; Presentment of the clerk of the Market against alehouse keepers 1708.

Colchester Borough Sessions records
Original recogs 1599-1604; Sessions Rolls contain some petitions, presentments etc concerning alehouses 1562-1700, incomplete; Regs of alehouse keepers c.1553-c.1562, 1599-1604, 1648-1689; Original recogs 1801-1829; Victuallers' regs 1764-1820; Certs of good character 1778-1790, 1799-1829 (incomplete); Interim licences 1764, 1799.

Petty Sessions records
Tendring PS Division: List of alehouse lics granted 1816.

1828 on: Inns, Public Houses and Beer Shops

Quarter Sessions records
Lic Ctee 1873-1939.
Reg of licences extinguished 1905-7.

Petty Sessions records
Becontree Div: Reg of lics, alehouses and beerhouses 1872-1972; Applications for alterations 1899-1944; Chairman's album of newspaper cuttings relating to Becontree Brewster Sessions 1882-1907; MS calendar incl. Special Sessions for transferring alehouse lics 1829; Lic plans, Becontree Div. 1899-1944.
Billericay Div: Reg of lics, incl. convictions against licensees 1947-55.
Brentwood Div: Reg of lics, incl. convictions, corres 1911-64; Lists of alehouse, beerhouse and wine lics 1923/26/27.
Chelmsford Div: Regs of lics, 1872-1960, incl. indexes .

Petty Sessions continued
Dengie Div: Regs of lics, 1872-1939.
Harwich Div: Regs of lics (and mins.?), 1940-86.
Liberty of Havering-atte-Bower: Reg of lics, very detailed 1872-1903.
Freshwell Div: Mins, lic meetings, 1830-1866; Reg of licences, 1879-1902, incl. owners' names.
Maldon Borough Div: Reg of lics, incl. convictions etc 1874-1938.
North Hinckford Div: Regs of lics, 1907-61.
Ongar Div: Mins 1829-36; lics reg, 1880-1901, 1907-1909.
Orsett Div: Regs of lics 1872-1903, c.1935-1959.
Romford Div: Regs of lics, 1903-1954.
Saffron Walden Borough: Regs of lics, 1899-1902, 1914-56.
Saffron Walden Dvi: Regs of lics. c.1960-84.
South Hinckford Div: Mins, 1825-28, 1832-72; Reg of lics, 1879-1902; 1924-43; Lic Returns, 1879, 1883, 1887-1903.
Halstead Bench: Regs of lics, 1914-60.
Walde Div: Regs of lics, 1916-60.
Witham Div: Mins, lic sessions 1824-1927 (incomplete and some fragile and closed).

Colchester Petty Sessions records
Registers of victuallers' licences: Harwich (Tendring) 1872-1910; Tendring (Clacton-on-Sea) 1915-60; Colchester PS Div 1872-1969; Lexden and Winstree 1911-69; Tendring 1894-1928.

Other Licences
Petty Sessions records
Brentwood Div: List of alehouse, beerhouse and wine licences 1923/26/27.

Other licences
Colchester Petty Sessions records:
Music and dancing lics: Colchester PS Div 1940-53.

1828 on: Inns, Public Houses and Beer Shops
Reg of alehouse, beer house and off licences: West Ham 1872-1904.

Other licensing activities
Council mins contain lics for music, dancing and stage plays: East Ham 1916-c.1960; West Ham 1898-c.1960.

Sandwich QS records, licensed victuallers' recognizances, 1636-1807, include a few for Brightlingsea.

GLOUCESTERSHIRE and BRISTOL

Boroughs which were their own licensing authority:
Gloucester, Bristol.

National records (see pages 6-8)

Letters Patent (1554-71): Bristol, Gloucester,
Tewkesbury, Thornbury.

Vintners' fines (1569-72): Bristol, Dursley,
Gloucester, Minchinhampton, Shirehampton,
Tetbury, Tewkesbury, Winchcombe, Wotton.

Victuallers' (Lenten) Recognizances (1572-1634).

Raleigh Wine Licences (1582-8, 1596-7).
For Bristol, see Somerset.

Mompesson Licences (1620): Almondesbury, Aust,
Bishops Cleeve, Bitton, Borton Regis (?),
Burbanke(?), Charlton, Coleford, Didmarton,
Dursley, Falfield, Frampton on Severn, Hambrook,
Huntley, Lydney, Minchinhampton, Newnham,
Tetbury, Thornbury, Wheatenhurst (Whitminster),
Winterbourne, Woodmancott, Wotton under Edge.
For Bristol see Somerset.

Coventry Wine Licences (1626-39): Beoley,
Berkeley, Bishops Cleeve, Bitton, Cheltenham,
Chipping Campden, Didmarton, Fremapton,
Frocester, Gloucester, Painswick, Stow on the
Wold, Stroud, Tewesbury.
For Bristol, see Somerset

Wine Licences: Pipe Office (1670-1756).

Gloucestershire Archives, Gloucester.

1552-1828: Inns and Alehouses

Quarter Sessions records
Indictment books incl keeping unlicensed ale-houses
1660-68, 1770-73, 1808-1910; Order books incl
orders for suppression of superfluous and
disorderly alehouses 1672 onwards; Original
recogs, 1755; Bisley Hundred 1781.

Gloucester Borough records
Regs of alehouses 1674-1836; Subscriptions by
licensees to orders and regulations for keeping
alehouses 1747-57; List of petitioners for lics 1756;
Petition for renewal of licences 1801-11.

1828 on: Inns, Public Houses and Beer Shops

Quarter Sessions records
Lic ctee mins 1874-89; County Council lic ctee mins
1934-64; Maps showing distribution of PHs in parts
of county and plans for building alterations, 1872-
1948; Notice of application for wine lic in
Cheltenham 1873; Notebook of chairman of lic
ctee 1905; Corres, compensation for closed
houses 1911; List of licensed houses, names of
occupiers, owners etc 1891 and 1903; Licensing
Act 1904; Report of lic ctee and Supplemental
report 1904 +1905; Lic papers 1904-44, 1946-56;
Parliamentary returns re licensing 1831-1897.

Petty Sessions records
Berkeley Div: Reg of lics 1903-63; Lic corres 1957-
1958; Papers re licensing 2 PHs 1957-9; Plans,
alteration of Salutation Inn, Ham 1963.

Gloucestershire Archives continued

Petty Sessions continued.
Campden Div: Reg of alehouse lics 1954-80.
Cheltenham Div: Reg of alehouse lics 1874-1930.
Cirencester: Regs of alehouse lics 1872-1925; Plans
of alterations to lic'd houses 1901-30; Mins of
Special Sessions 1902-64; Lists of lic'd houses
1897-1903.
Coleford Div: Reg of alehouse lics 1907-47.
Dursley Div: Regs of lics 1872-1900, 1903-63;
Applications for off-licences; Sessions papers;
Papers re licensing 1957-60; Plans of alehouses
1904-27, and petition re numbers of alehouses ;
Architects' plans of alterations 1934-58.
Fairford Div: Regs of alehouses 1872-1973;
Licensing papers from 1873.
Gloucester City Div: Reg of alehouses 1954-67.
Gloucester County Division: Regs of alehouses
1872-1965; Licensing papers 1821-50.
Lawford's Gate Div: Regs of alehouses 1826-1944,
1954-63; Mins of lic JPs 1903-44; Beerhouse
informations 1840-51, 1862-65.
Moreton-in-Marsh Div: Reg of lics 1872-1934.
Nailsworth Div: Reg of alehouse lics 1903-53.
Newent Div: Regs of alehouses 1903-37, 1949,
1872-1977; Mins of annual lic meetings 1908-59.
Newnham Div: Reg of alehouse lics 1869-1973.
Northleach Div: Reg of alehouse lics 1935-55.
Stroud Div: Reg of lics 1925-57.
Chipping Sodbury Div: Reg of lics 1939-63.
Stow-on-the-Wold Div: Reg of alehouse lics 1902,
1906-76.
Tewkesbury Div: Regs of alehouse lics 1872-1953.
Whitminster Div: Reg of lics 1872-1962; Lic papers
1870-1915, 1957-63; Lists of alehouse lics granted
1869-1872; Evidence of various alehouses, 1905;
Plans of alehouses 1906-1921.
Winchcombe Div: Reg of alehouse lics 1903-76.
Wotton-under-Edge Div: Regs of lics 1913-63.

Gloucester Borough records
Returns of constables as to the state of public
houses during times of divine services 1836.

Bristol Record Office.

1552-1828: Inns and Alehouses

Bristol records
Presentments to Grand Juries, incl selling without
licence etc 1628-1666, 1676-1700.
Licences to alehouse keepers 1654-63, 1666-1700,
1701-62 (incl convictions for unlicensed houses),
1763-76, 1796-1814.
Reg of all innkeepers, vintners etc in Bristol, listed in
wards, with note of moneys collected 1802-8 and list
of all innkeepers and inns in each ward 1809-11.
Reg of halliers, brewers and glassmakers 1718-56.
Town Clerk's Boxes of official papers include lists of
alehouses and inns prepared by ward constables
in connection with licensing 1752-64.

Quarter Sessions records
Lists of unlicensed ale sellers, nine wards 1718-19.
Lists of licensed alehouses 1760.

Gloucestershire: *Bristol Record Office*, continued

1828 on: Inns, Public Houses and Beer Shops

Bristol Quarter Sessions records
Information re inns and alehouses 1834-35.

Bristol Magistrates' Court records
Regs of lics for beer houses 1869-79; Reg of lics granted to keepers of wine and beer houses, and of transfers of lics 1875-89; Regs of beerhouses, grocers' and dealers' lics 1879-1951; Regs of lics granted to inns, alehouses and victualling houses 1872-1924; Regs of transfers of lics and grants of special lics 1886-98.

Licensing Committee records
Mins 1889-1944; Compensation Authority ctee mins 1904-30.

Bristol Magistrates' Court records
Regs of persons convicted as habitual drunkards 1903-4; Newscuttings 1885-1906.

Bristol Constabulary records
Alehouse and beerhouse complaints; many include notes of Brewster and Transfer Sessions, arranged in five divisions, A, B, C, D and H, 1895-1970.
Reg of beerhouse keepers, *c.*1841-1897, includes spirit and wine lic holders in C Division.
Plan of alteration of beerhouse approved by police superintendent, 1903.

Other licences
Form of licence under Public Health Acts Amendment Act 1890 - Music and Dancing, 1950s.

HAMPSHIRE

Boroughs which were their own licensing authority:
Andover, Basingstoke, Lymington, Romsey, Southampton, Winchester.
Licensing Divisions post-1828 include:
Alresford, Alton, Andover, Basingstoke, Christchurch (now in Dorset), Droxford, Eastleigh, Fareham, Gosport, Havant, Kingsclere, Lymington, New Forest, Odiham (later Aldershot), Petersfield, Ringwood, Southampton (later renamed Eastleigh), Winchester.

Hampshire continued

National records (see pages 6-8)

Letters Patent (1554-71): Andover, Basingstoke, Hursley, Newport, Odiham, Romsey, Southampton, Whitchurch, Winchester.
Vintners' fines (1569-72): Alton, Andover, Basingstoke, Christchurch, Hartley Row, Havant, Petersfield, Portsmouth, Romsey, Southampton, Titchfield, Winchester.
Victuallers' (Lenten) Recognizances (1572-1634).
Raleigh Wine Licences (1582-7, 1595-7).
Mompesson Licences (1620): Alresford, Alton, Andover, Basingstoke, Bishops Waltham, Botley, Brockenhurst, Brook, Buriton, Catherington, Fareham, Fordingbridge, Gosport, Hambledon, Hartley Wintney, Havant, Hinton Ampner, Hook Street(?), Hursley, Hurstbourne Tarrant, Kingsclere, Liss, Longstone(?), Milton, Minstead, Newport, Overton, Pawton(?), Pilley (Boldre), Purwell Street (Christchurch), Ringwood, St. Mary Bourne, Selborne, Sherborne (St. John), Southampton, Stockbridge, North and South Warnborough, Whitchurch, Winchester, Soke of Winchester, Winchester Street (Andover), Yarmouth.
Coventry Wine Licences (1626-39): Cowes, Gosport, Lymington, Newchurch in Whippingham, Portsmouth, East Tisted, Southampton, Stockbridge and Hursley, Warnford, Winchester.
Wine Licences: Pipe Office (1670-1756).

Hampshire Record Office, *Winchester.*

1552-1828: Inns and Alehouses

Quarter Sessions records
A few original recogs are found in the following records: Sessions Rolls - Misc Files, 1658; QS Order Books 1607-27; QS Mins 1559-77, 1624-1634; Sessions Rolls - Indictment.
Order Books (1628 onwards) and Mins contain some general statements re licensing and re neglect and destruction of recogs 1736 and 1787.
Sessions Rolls - Indictments contain petitions, presentments and indictments re alehouses.
List of innkeepers and victuallers, Fawley Division 1745; Collection of alehouse lics 1715-29; List of lics granted for Andover, Fawley and Portsdown Divs 1710-1727.

Borough records
Andover: Some alehouse lics, petitions etc for 17th and 18th centuries.
Basingstoke: Alehouse lics 1618, 1727-30; Lists of alehouses 1660-63, 1712-19; Excise proceedings 1740-48.
Lymington: Mins, 1593-1648, list of victuallers' lics.
Winchester: Victuallers' recogs 1646, 1713-1808.

1828 on: Inns, Public Houses and Beer Shops

Quarter Sessions records
Order books: general orders and appeals re lics.

Hampshire: *County Record Office,* continued

Other County records
Confirming and compensation ctee plans 1896-1961;
County lic ctee, confirming and compensation ctee
section mins 1904-71; Correspondence re lic
restrictions 1915.

Petty Sessions records
Minute books post-1872 for various Divisions contain
information on licensing.
Fareham Petty Sessions Div Minute books before
1872 contain details of beer house licences.
Winchester City: Mins of lic JPs, 1903-6, 1912-1920;
Schedules of lic'd premises, 1907-8; Applications
for lics, 1918-19.
Registers of Victuallers' lics (by Div or Borough):
Alton 1903-1970; Fareham 1872-1927; Gosport
1925-1939; Havant 1913-1964; New Forest 1930-
1945; Odiham (later Aldershot) 1873-1962;
Petersfield 1935-62; Ringwood 1892-1962;
Romsey Borough 1952-65; Romsey (Div) 1922-
1965; Southampton (later Eastleigh) 1872-1920;
Totton and New Forest 1946-67.

Licences for other activities
Music and dancing lics, Havant 1948-63.

Isle of Wight County Record Office, *Newport.*

Newport Borough records
One bundle of certificates, 1674-1885, including
licences for alehouses, dating from 1751 but
particularly for the year 1833.

Southampton Archives.

1552-1828: Inns and Alehouses
Borough Sessions
Order Books (1609 onwards) and Sessions Rolls
(1622 -1843) are likely to contain refs; Reg of
alehouse keepers 1661-1668; Court leet records
1549 to date contain indictments against disorderly
alehouses; List of licensed victuallers 1797; Certs
granting right to keep PH *c.*1820 .

1828 on: Inns, Public Houses and Beer Shops
Lists of lic'd victuallers 1829-1835; Draft summons
for alehouse keepers 1829; List of those applying
for lics 1832; Lists of lic'd premises 1915, 1934.

Magistrates' court records
Regs of lics 1900, 1903-23; *General & on-lics:* Regs
of lics (full, off & beer) 1941-57; Reg of full on-lics
1941-66; Files on-lics lapsed etc 1941-66; On-lic
with lic histories back to 1940s, c.1966-95. Lic
compensation authority mins 1905-32; Reg of lics
referred 1904-1910; Mins, lic matters, incl compensation and consolidation 1904-59, 1987-94.

Licences for other activities
Music, singing and dancing lics, 1947-9, 1959-1960;
Music and dancing 1940-49; Reg of music, singing
and dancing lics 1950-56; Bookmakers and
gaming permits 1970-95; Reg of Clubs 1941-96.

HEREFORDSHIRE
Boroughs which were their own licensing authority:
Hereford.
Licensing Divisions post-1828:
Abbey Dore, Bredwardine, Bromyard, Harewood
End, Hereford, Kington, Ledbury, Leominster,
Ross, Weobley, Wigmore.

National records (see pages 6-8)

Letters Patent (1554-71): Hereford.
Vintners' fines (1569-72): Ledbury.
Victuallers' (Lenten) Recognizances (1572-1634).
Raleigh Wine Licences (1582-4, 1587-8, 1595-6).
Mompesson Licences (1620): Goodrich, Ross.
Coventry Wine Licences (1626-39): Hereford,
Leominster.
Wine Licences: Pipe Office (1670-1756).

Herefordshire Archive Service, *Hereford.*

1552-1828: Inns and Alehouses

Quarter Sessions records
Lists of licences granted at Ledbury 1790.
Alehouse keepers' recognizances at Ledbury 1795.
Alehouse keepers' recognizances registered in
enrolment book, by hundred, 1818-1870.
Certificate of licences granted at Kington and
Huntington hundreds 1796.

Hereford City Quarter Sessions records
Recognizances 1605-1757.
Recognizance rolls 1822, 1822-28.

1828 on: Inns, Public Houses and Beer Shops

Quarter Sessions records
Alehouse keepers' recogs registered in enrolment
book, by hundred, 1818-1870.
Regs of lics: Bromyard PS Div 1959-75; Weobley PS
Div 1903-31; Dore PS Div 1872-1900.
Petitions for pub licence renewals 1899-1901.
Plan of Hereford indicating lic'd houses1887-91.
Corres file 1937-38, incl corres on licensing in
Hereford.
'Hereford Times' County Council and Brewster
Sessions Supplement Feb. 1903.
Magistrates licensing regs, 1872-1978.
Licensing Committee records, 1872-1904.
Return of licensed houses, 1903-1905.
Objections against valuations, 1925-41.
Herefordshire Magistrates Court lic regs, mainly
1962-86, some from 1928 and some to 1996.
List of licensed premises, 1982.

Police records
Return of licensed premises for Herefordshire, 1905,
printed.
Reports of Chief Constable to QS 1894-1939.

Hereford City Quarter Sessions records
Reg of lics, Hereford City 1872-77, 1891-1903.
Plans of licensed houses 1905-40.

HERTFORDSHIRE

Boroughs which were their own licensing authority: St. Albans.

National records (see pages 6-8)

Letters Patent (1554-71): Barnet, Hoddesdon, Much Hadham, Royston, St. Albans, Ware, Waltham Cross, Welwyn.
Vintners' fines (1569-72): Baldock, Barnet, Berkhamstead, Bishops Stortford, Buntingford, Hadham, Hemel Hempstead, Hertford, Hitchin, Puckeridge, Ware, Watford.
Victuallers' (Lenten) Recognizances (1572-1634).
Raleigh Wine Licences (1582-5, 1589-90, 1591-2, 1593-7).
Mompesson Licences (1620): Abbots Langley, Baldock, Barkway, Bishops Hatfield, Bishops Stortford, Broxbourne, Buntingford, Bushey, Cheston(?), Cheston Street(?), Chipping Barnet, Elstree, (Kings) Hatfield, Hemel Hempstead, Hitchin, Hoddesdon, (London) Colney, Much Hadham, Park Street(?), Pirton, Puckeridge, Royston, St. Albans, Sandon, Sandridge, Sawbridgeworth, Shenley, Tring, Turners Hill(?), Waade Mill(?), Walkern, Waltham Cross, Watford, Watton at Stone, Welwyn, Wheathampstead.
Coventry Wine Licences (1626-39): Baldock, Barkway, Bishops Hatfield, Bishops Stortford, Buntingford, Much Hadham, Hemel Hempstead, Hitchin, Market Street, Rickmansworth, Sawbridgeworth, Watford, Wormley.
Wine Licences: Pipe Office (1670-1756).
Military Survey 1756 (see page 11). St Albans District: places, names of victuallers and signs, numbers of beds and stabling [WO 30/49, ff.68-71]; Ware, Enfield (incl. Epping, Wareham, Barnet, Cheshunt, Tottenham), places of abode, signs, beds and stabling [WO.30/49, ff.73-78]; Uxbridge District (incl. Watford, Beaconsfield, Rickmansworth, Edgware), places, names, signs, beds and stabling [WO 30/49 ff.80-83].

Hertfordshire Archives & Local Studies, Hertford.

1552-1828: Inns and Alehouses

County Quarter Sessions records
Sessions rolls include articles and orders as to alehouses, recognizances, petitions for renewing licences, orders for suppressions of licences, complaints as to and prosecutions relating to disorderly or unlicensed alehouses 1581-1698.
Sessions books include articles and orders as to alehouses, recognizances, grants of licences, petitions for licences, suppressions of licences, prosecutions concerning disorderly or unlicensed alehouses, 1619-1828.
Reg of victuallers' recognizances for whole county excepting the Liberty of St. Albans 1817-1828.
Memorandum of victuallers' recognizances made at Royston for parishes in Odsey Hundred 1712.

Hertfordshire Archives continued

Copy list of victuallers' recogs taken at Hatfield, covering parishes of Hatfield, Totteridge, Welwyn, Ayot St. Lawrence, Shenley, North Mimms 1824.
Victuallers' recognizances for Hundreds of Braughing, Broadwater, Dacorum, Edwinstree, Hertford, Hitchin, and Odsey 1806-28.
List of alehouses at Hertford, Cheshunt, Brickendon, Great Amwell, Liberty of Bailey Hall, and Hoddesdon 1596-7.
Liberty of St. Albans Quarter Sessions records
Register of victuallers' recognizances 1822-1828.
Victuallers' recognizances 1786-1825.

Petty Sessions records
Barnet Division: Court mins incl annual lic sessions of the Liberty of St. Albans for Chipping Barnet, East Barnet, Elstree, Northaw, Ridge 1750-97.
Dacorum Division: Court mins incl grants of alehouse lics for 1820-21.
Hitchin Division: Court mins incl grants of alehouse lics 1808-25.

Hertford Borough records
Books of recognizances dealt with at Petty Sessions 1623-37, 1716-1820; Reg of victuallers' recogs 1824-25; Victuallers' recogs and alehouse lics 1779-1828; Lists of inns, innkeepers and their sureties 1623-47, 1710-85.

Other non-offical records
Grants of lics 1662 [29142]; Recogs 1754-58 [12142-64]; Petition concerning disorderly alehouse at Rickmansworth; 1588 [8430]; Schedules of innkeepers 1627-28 [40842-6].

1828 on: Inns, Public Houses and Beer Shops

Liberty of St. Albans Quarter Sessions records
Minutes of the Licensing Committee 1873-97.

Police records
Register of public, beer, wine, refreshment, and lodging houses 1884-1962.

County Quarter Sessions records
Sessions books include prosecutions for offences contrary to alehouse recognizances 1828-43.
Appointment of special licensing sessions to be held in the various hundreds 1828.
Misc papers about licensing inns, 1869-78.
Mins of County Lic Ctee 1873-94 and Hertford Div and St. Albans Div Lic Ctees 1897-1951.
Notebooks of the chairman of the Assessment Appeals and Licensing Ctees 1925-40.
Licensing Area maps for the county 1902.

Petty Sessions records
Registers of alehouse lics: Albury Div 1872-1953; Barnet Div 1872-1964; Bishops Stortford Div 1922-1959; Buntingford Div 1946-59; Cheshunt Div 1931-39; Dacorum Div 1901-63; Hatfield Div 1893-1902; Hertford Borough Div 1903-66; Hertford County Div 1903-66; Hitchin Div 1872-1953; South Mimms Div 1939-65; Odsey Div 1872-1953; St. Albans City Div 1900-75; Stevenage Div 1897-1954;

Hertfordshire: *Archives & Local Studies,* contd.

Ware Div 1872-1966; Watford Div 1874-1951; Welwyn Div 1899-1955.
Mins of annual lic meetings for St. Albans City Div 1902-70.
Clerk's list of lic'd victuallers for Ware Div 1851.

Other non-official records
Solicitors' papers concerning licensing applications c.1870-92 [D/EL 2199, 2754-5, 2986-7, 3002-7, 3871].
Applications for PH licences and beer certificates in parish papers 1830-44 [D/P37/29/3; D/P24A/10/1].

Other licences

County Quarter Sessions records
Papers re music and dancing lics 1867 and 1893.

Liberty of St. Albans Quarter Sessions records
Grants of music and dancing lics 1836-40.

Petty Sessions records
Hitchin Div: regs of music and dancing lics 1912-33.

Central Library, St. Albans.

Calendar of victuallers' recognizances 1822-28.

Note. No relevant records at *Barnet Archives and Local Studies Department.*

HUNTINGDONSHIRE

National records (see pages 6-8)

Letters Patent (1554-71): Huntingdon, Spaldwick, St. Ives, St. Neots.
Vintners' fines (1569-72): None.
Victuallers' (Lenten) Recognizances (1572-1634).
Raleigh Wine Licences (1582-7).
Mompesson Licences (1620): Alconbury, St. Ives, St. Neots, Yaxley.
Coventry Wine Licences (1626-39): Huntingdon, St Ives, St Neots, Fen Stanton
Wine Licences: Pipe Office (1670-1756).

Huntingdonshire Archives, Huntingdon.

1552-1828: Inns and Alehouses

Quarter Sessions records
Sessions papers include depositions etc concerning licensing matters 1788 onwards.
Victuallers' register, Hurstingstone Hundred 1788.

Huntingdon Borough records
Recognizances 1823-28; Sessions mins with reg information 1754-75 [all unfit for use at present].
A single stray county recognzance of 1805 [H3/2].

1828 on: Inns, Public Houses and Beer Shops

Quarter Sessions records
Sessions papers include some licensing matters but only convictions have been catalogued.

Huntingdonshire: *Hunts. Archives* continued

County records
County Licence Committee mins 1873-1904; Compensation Committee mins 1904-47; Compensation Commitee letter books 1911-57.
Petty Sessions records
Registers of licences: Godmanchester Borough PS Div 1872-1901; Huntingdon Borough PS Div 1872-1955; Huntingdon PS Div 1955-95; Hurstingstone PS Div 1903-09; Leightonstone PS Div 1890-1957; Norman Cross PS Div 1872-78; Peterborough PS Div 1983; Ramsey PS Div 1907-10, 1925-38, 1940s-1979; St. Ives PS Div 1875-1902; St. Neots PS Division 1981; Toseland PS Division 1947-49.

Borough records
Godmanchester: Lic Ctee mins 1848-52.
Huntingdon: Letters 1842 re alteration of licensing rules under 1840 Act.

Other records
Huntingdon Borough and Leightonstone PS Div: Papers including notices to apply for lics, surveyors' reports 1950-56, lic plans 1938-1956.

KENT

Boroughs which were their own licensing authority: Liberty of Romney Marsh, Sandwich, Tenterden.
Licensing Districts, post-1828: Ashford Division, Dartford Division, Malling Division, North Aylesford Division, Home Division, Seven Oaks Division, Sittingbourne Division, Tonbridge Division, Wingham Division, New Romney.

National records (see pages 6-8)

Letters Patent (1554-71): Canterbury, Cranbrook, Deptford, East Greenwich, Greenwich, Gravesend.
Vintners' fines (1569-72): Canterbury, Hawkhurst, Maidstone, Rochester.
Victuallers' (Lenten) Recognizances (1572-1634).
Raleigh Wine Licences (1582-8, 1591-4, 1595-7).
Mompesson Licences (1620): Ash, Ashford, Benenden, Bersted, Bromley, Brookland, Canterbury, Chalk, Cranbrook, Eastry, Ewell, Eythorn, East Greenwich, Hawkhurst, Ickham, Lenham, Littlebourne, "(Town)" Malling, Margate, Milton, Pluckley, Rochester, Rolvenden, Saltwood, Sandhurst, Sevenoaks, Smarden, Southend(?), Staple, Thanet, Tonbridge, Warden, Westerham, West Wickham, Wingham.
Coventry Wine Licences (1626-39): Ash, Aveley, Aylesford, Bexley and Foots Cray, Biddenden and Appledore, Bromley, Canterbury, Chipstead, Dartford, Deptford, Dover, Egerton, Eltham, Erith, Faversham, Gravesend, Greenwich, Highgate, Kenthatch, Limberowe and Minster, Maidstone, Marden, Margate, Ramsgate, Rochester, New Romney, Sandway, Sandwich, Seal, Sittingbourne, Strood, Tonbridge, Wellinge, Westerham.
Wine Licences: Pipe Office (1670-1756).

Kent continued

1552-1828: Inns and Alehouses

County Quarter Sessions records
Sessional Rolls, 1600 onwards includes lists of
victuallers presentments, informations etc.
Session Papers, includes lic papers from 1660.
Original recognizances, 1649-1752.
Annual lists and register: Blackheath Div 1710-13,
1717, 1726; Dartford Div 1707; Rochester Div
1710-15; Sevenoaks Div c.1750; Home Div 1727-
1773; Wingham Div 1736-73.
Registers of alehouse keepers 1753-1827.
Annual draft registers 1766-71, 1790.

Borough records
Faversham: Victuallers' recognizances 1570-1835.
Maidstone: Victuallers' recognizances 1651-85,
1747-61, 1822-28.
Liberty of Romney Marsh Court of Quarter Sessions:
Special and PS papers incl lic matters 1710-1851.
Sandwich Court of Quarter Sessions: Licensed
victuallers' recognizances 1635-1807 including
Ramsgate, Sarre, Deal, Walmer, Brighton.
Tenterden Court of Quarter Sessions:
Victuallers' recognizance rolls 1676-1706.

1828 on: Inns, Public Houses and Beer Shops

County Quarter Sessions records
Reg of beer shop certs 1840-43; Original certs of
ratable value of beer shops 1840-3; Lic Ctee
Papers incl Mins (1872-1933); list of lics referred to
under 1904 Act (1905-13); lic rules (1905); certs of
lics granted under 1910 Consolidation Act (1918-
1931); agenda book (1926-1934); chairmen's
notebooks (1913-37); Mins or Order Books: formal
minutes incl. those of Lic Ctees (1931 onwards).

Borough records: See above for Romney Marsh.

Petty Sessions Records
Registers of licences: Dartford Div 1872-1924;
Malling Div 1879-1903; Sittingborne Div 1908-
1912; Wingham Div 1872-1902 (extracts only).
Certs on behalf of petitioners for lics: Home Div
1753-1775.
Mins of Special Sessions for licensing: New Romney
1868-1893.

Estate and Family Papers
Dodwell Collection, includes list of Maidstone inns
with signs and names of licensees, 1610 [U47/45].
Knocker Collection, includes amongst the official
papers, licensing papers for Quarter and General
Sessions 1820-63 [U55].

Other licences

Sandwich Borough Records
Licensed wine retailers for a short period following
the 1553 Act [Sa/AC 4 fo 300v].

County Council Committee records
Minutes of music and dancing lic ctee 1894-1933,
1955-74. See General Purposes Committee.

North Aylesford Petty Sessional Division (magistrates
court) [PSNA] on mf and digitised online:
<http://cityark.medway.gov.uk>
Licensing registers. 1872-1960 [PSNA 88-144].
Beer and wine lics 1869-1937 [PSNA 145-184].
List of alehouses & applications to keep ale, 1890-
1937 [PSNA 185-223].
Estate Papers: Rogers, Stevens & Chance, public
house and hotel valuers, 1923-80 [DE852, 1102].
Also breweries throughout Kent. Listing in progress
Best family of Chatham and Boxley, family, estate
and brewery business records. 1820s [U480].
Hulkes (formerly Wildash) of Chatham, brewers
[DE505, DE528].
Winch & Winch of Chatham, solicitors, clients'
records incl. Dartford Brewery Co. and Style &
Winch, brewers [14E].
Budden & Biggs Brewery Ltd, Strood, brewers and
wine and spirit merchants [DE876].
Dove, Phillips & Pett, of Strood and Rochester,
mineral water manufacturers [U1782].
Also many local authority building plans and photos
for Medway Towns, c.1850-1974.

Victuallers' recogs of 41 licensees in the parishes of
Eynsford, Farningham, Horton Kirby, Kingsdown,
Southfleet, Sutton at Hone, Swanscombe, Eltham,
Beckenham, Bromley, Plumstead, Bexley,
Chelsfield, Chislehurst, Foots Cray, St Mary Cray,
Cudham, Downe, and Orpington, 1605.

Petty Sessions records
Bromley PS minute books 1747-87.

Blackheath Hundred justices' minutes 1743-1909
(microfilm). No other relevant records.

Note. No relevant records held at *Bexley Libraries
and Museums Department.*

LANCASHIRE

Licensing Districts post-1828
Boroughs: Accrington, Ashton-under-Lyne, Barrow in
Furness, Blackburn, Bolton, Bootle, Burnley, Bury,
Clitheroe, Colne, Darwen, Eccles, Heywood,
Lancaster, Leigh, Liverpool, Manchester,
Middleton, Morecambe, Mossley, Nelson, Oldham,
Preston, Rochdale, St. Helens, Salford, Southport,
Warrington, Wigan.
County Divisions: Accrington, Ashton-under-Lyne,
Blackburn, Bolton, Burnley, Bury, Childwall,
Church, Clitheroe, Colne, Darwen, Garstang,
Hawkshead, Hornby, Kirkdale, Kirkham, Leigh,
Leyland, Leyland Hundred, Manchester, Middleton,
North Lonsdale, Oldham, Ormskirk, Prescot,
Rossendale, St. Helens, South Lonsdale,
Southport, Walton-le-Dale, Warrington, Widnes.

Lancashire continued

National records (see pages 6-8)

Letters Patent (1554-71): None.
Vintners' fines (1569-74): Bolton, Garstang, Lancaster, Leigh, Liverpool, Newton, Ormskirk, Prescot, Preston, Warrington.
Victuallers' Recognizances (1572-1634): None.
Raleigh Wine Licences (1582-6, 1588-8, 1593-4, 1596-7).
Mompesson Licences (1620): None.
Coventry Wine Licences (1626-39): Bury, Clitheroe and Whalley, Dalton and Ulverston, Garstang, Lancaster, Poulton, Preston, Warrington.
Wine Licences: Pipe Office (1670-1756).

Lancashire Record Office, *Preston.*

1552-1828: Inns and Alehouses

Quarter Sessions records
Quarter Sessions Petitions contain lic records 1648-1908; Original recogs 1621-1828; Return of ale-house keepers, Blackburn Hundred 1655; Extracts of fines for alehouses 1650; Victuallers' regs 1822-1829; Licences and summons for selling ale without licence 1792-1835; Alehouse lics, Milnrow 1782, 1786 and for sale of wine and spirits

Clitheroe Borough records
Alehouse recognizances 1649-53.
Bolton: Restrictions on licensing, 1798.

1828 on: Inns, Public Houses and Beer Shops

Quarter Sessions records
Licensing Ctee mins: Lonsdale Hundred 1873-1974; Amounderness, Blackburn and Leyland Hundred 1873-1974; West Derby Hundred 1872-1974; Salford Hundred 1873-1974.
Returns of public houses 1890, 1904.
Licensing Compensation reports 1907-48

Petty Sessions records
Accrington. Reports and stats. 1961-64.
Amounderness Div: Regs 1896-1971.
Barrow in Furness Borough Div: Regs 1874-1949.
Blackburn Borough Div: Regs 1872-1932; Reg of lics refused 1905-10; Account book of charges under 1904 Licensing Act; Treasurer's account, Compensation Fund 1905-32; Seal matrix of licensing justices, n.d. ?19th century.
Blackburn County Div: Regs 1948-60; Court files incl lic applications 1949-67; Lic mins 1872-1934; Liquor licensing files 1953-62; Instalment regs, includes lists of PHs 1959-64; Plans of licensed premises *c.*1903-1960s.
Blackpool Borough: Licensing regs 1903-49.; stats. 1911-16.
Bolton by Bowland Div: Licensing regs 1903-74.
Bolton. Lic. regs 1872-1974; plans C20.
Burnley Borough: Licensing regs 1872-1977; Licensing plans.

Burnley Div: Licensing regs 1899-1954.
Burnley and Colne Div: Licensing regs 1955-59.
Church Div (amal with BlAckburn 1961): Court files incl lic applications 1953-60; Lic files 1944-60.
Clitheroe Borough: Licensing regs 1903-62.
Clitheroe Div: Licensing regs 1911-74.
Colne Borough: Licensing regs 1888-1951.
Colne Div: Lic regs 1906-54; Lic reports 1926-28.
Darwen Div (amal with Blackburn 1967): Court files incl lic applications 1944-67; Lic mins 1881-1947; Regs of hotels and public houses 1923-65; Lic files, Compensation Authority 1904-31; Lic files, applications and statistics 1954-67; Papers re lic matters including plans 1947-53; Plans of licensed premises.
Garstang Div: Regs 1872-1957; Plans of lic premises.
Hornby Div (amalgamated with Lonsdale 1955, Lancaster 1974): Regs 1872-1957.
Kirkdale Div: Regs of licensed premises 1953-62 Plans of licensed premises 1903-59.
Kirkham. General lic meetings papers, 1946-59.
Lancaster Borough Div: Regs 1903-26, 1950-62.
Leyland and Leyland Hundred Div: Regs, all divs 1872-78; Regs, Chorley, Croston, Rufford, Standish 1878-1944; Regs, Leyland 1878-1922.
Middleton Borough Div: Reg of beer house convictions 1872-87.
Nelson Borough: Licensing reg 1893-1962 .
North Lonsdale Div: Regs 1872-1927.
South Lonsdale Div: Regs 1872-88, 1903-57.
Preston Borough Div: Regs 1969-92: Plans of lic'd premises; Compensation Authority mins and papers 1911-74; Chief Constables' reports 1910, 1912, 1914, 1915, 1920.
Rossendale Div: Regs of PHs in Bacup and Rawtenstall *c.*1870-1985; Inspection Ctee reports 1903-28; Returns and corres re licensing incl statistics 1909-64; plans 1959-78..
St. Helens Borough Div: Annual Lic Meeting mins 1903-15; Regs 1882-1937; Lists of lic'd victuallers 1882-92, 1897-1901; Annual statements of account 1906-15.
Walton-le-Dale Div: Reg 1932-60.

Other local authority records
Fleetwood MB: Notices to transfer lics of PHs etc 1916-17.
Rossendale Div: Annual reports and statistics to the General Annual Licensing Sessions 1896-1983.
Burnley Borough: Reg of beer sellers 1887-91; Reg of beerhouse keepers 1889-96; Reg of licensed victuallers 1890-23.
Wigan Borough: Annual reports to Gen. Annual Lic. Sessions 1930-69; Reg of licences 1921-64.
Preston Borough: Brewster Sessions (printed) 1916-45; licensing records, 1880s-1950s..

Police records
Chief constables' reports often contain licensing details and statistics - available for many borough forces.
Blackburn Borough Police alehouse licensing 1894-1971.

Lancashire: *Lancashire Record Office* continued

Licences for other activities

County Quarter Sessions records
Lics for the sale of tea, coffee and chocolate,
Milnrow 1810-11.

Wigan Borough: Reg of music and dancing lics
1933-53.

Cumbria Record Office, Barrow in Furness

Petty Sessions records
Barrow in Furness Division. Lic regs 1874-1939.
North Lonsdale Division. Lic regs 1874-1939.

Furness Collection: Petty Sessions records
North Lonsdale District:
    Files containing stray documents relating to the
licensing of about 50 inns and public houses 1850-
1881. Most are notices of intention to apply for a
licence, but there are a few petitions and testimonials and a small number of licences. Other
records include:
    Monthly retail beer licence lists sent to the North
    Lonsdale magistrates court 1855-60; Draft
    minutes of licensing meeting 1885; Return to
    the House of Commons 1883, statistical; Two
    files relating to annual lic meetings 1857, 1859.
Hawkshead District: Correspondence file of clerk of
court, 1919.

Bolton Museum and Archive Service.

Bolton Borough Magistrates' Court records
Lic mins of annual General Lic Meetings and Special
Lic Meetings, 4 vols 1863-1920 (contain details of
applications, transfers and renewals); Innkeepers'
lic reg (includes names and addresses, details of
transfers, convictions etc) 1877-1962; three vols
Beerhouse lic regs, transfers c.1877-90;
Beerhouse lic reg (full information as above)
c.1894-1960; Beerhouse lic register (full
information) c.1877-1917; Beer off-licence reg (full
information) 1898-1962; Reg of lics referred (1904
Licensing Act) (names and addresses,
compensation paid etc) 1905-34; Reg of lics
extinguished 1905-68; Maps and plans of licensed
premises in Bolton, 1872-1975 (detailed list and
index available).

Other licences
Bolton Borough Magistrates' Court records
Reg of lics, billiards, bowls, bagatelle, table tennis,
music and dancing in Borough of Bolton 1904-58.

Bolton Borough Police archives
Lic plans of inns, beer houses, hotels etc c.1910-80.

Greater Manchester Record Office.

Petty Sessions records
Bury Borough: Lic Ctee Ms 1920-66; Lic certs 1844-
1965; Lic regs 1872-1943.
Heywood Borough: Court registers incl Transfer
Sessions 1913-55.

Greater Manchester Record Office continued

Bury County: Lic regs 1903.
Oldham Borough: Court regs including Transfer
    Sessions; Maps and plans of PHs submitted to the
    court 1939-74.
Saddleworth: Reg of licences 1894-1945.
Trafford (now at Sale):
    Altrincham. Public houses, 1939-51, 1953-70s;
    Clubs, 1961-74; Licensing committee 1968-75.
    Strangeways. Public House, 1872-84, 1925-63;
    Clubs, 1963-1970s. Plans C19 and C20.

Other licences

Reg of licences for public dancing, singing and
music (may include PHs) 1890-1926.
Music licensing register: Bury Borough 1893-1946;
Bury County 1948-66.

Manchester Central Library, Local Studies Unit.

1552-1828: Inns and Alehouses

Petition of James Denney to mayor of Liverpool
against refusal of magistrates to renew his licence
for James Street Tavern 1815 [MISC/672/6].

1828 on: Inns, Public Houses and Beer Shops

Manchester Petty Sessions records
Licensing convictions 1849, 1861-72, 1888-1908.

Registers: Clubs c.1903-62; Beerhouses etc 1869-71
(alphabetical by licensee); Beer, wine, spirits,
liquer & sweets retailers 1872-73, 1875-1909 (by
police district, street name); Licensed premises
1900-03; Licensed victuallers 1888-1909;
Licensing 1889-1960 (by police district, street
name); Music, dancing & rooms 1880s-1927,
transfers 1903-62;
Applications for music exemptions 1945-58; Special
sessions for granting music etc lics 1933-62;
Alehouse lics transfers 1930-61; Surrender of lics
1894-1927; Special exemptions 1945-64;
Occasional lic & exemptions 1950-65; Reg of
licensing complaints 1922-50; Reg of licensed
premises in Burnage, Didsbury, Moss Side,
Withington etc on accession to City of Manchester
1904-05; Licensing compensation authority letter
book 1919-35; Comp authority receipts/payments
1905-43; list of lics referred to Comp Ctee 1938;
Summons reg 1938; Reg of moneylenders 1927-
1950; Reg of billiard lics c1886-c1937;
Lic meetings mins 1874-81; General annual lic
meeting mins 1882-1911; Lic Ctee mins 1903-66;
Lic Ctee fil 1929-32; Lic Planning Ctee mins 1960-
1966; Betting lics Ctee mins 1960-67.

Other licences
Tobacco licences, Manchester, 1808 [MISC/672/3],
    1810 to James Denney (see above) [MISC/672/5].
Retail spirit licence for innkeeper of the Volunteer,
    Manchester (also link with above) [MISC/672/4].

Lancashire continued

Liverpool City Library,
Record Office & Local History Department.

Regs of alehouse lics, 56 vols. 1842-1930; Regs of wine and beer house certs, 5 vols 1869-1874; Reg of wine dealers' lics 1903-30; Reg of transfers and applications (for lics for victuallers, beer retailers, and others) 1901-1919; Newscuttings on lics; Lic plans, 7 documents 1887-1914; Misc papers, 1 vol 1852-1951; Special Meeting mins 1836.

Wigan Archives Service, Leigh.

1552-1828: Inns and Alehouses

Borough records
Wigan Borough Court Leet roll 1634 contains a list of alehouses; Wigan Borough QS, contains a very few lists of alehouse keepers 1733-1971.

Family records
Grimshaw Papers, papers of Thomas Grimshaw, town clerk and clerk of the peace for Wigan, contain lists of licensed alehouses in Wigan Borough 1807-35 [D/DX Ap G].

1828 on: Inns, Public Houses and Beer Shops

Petty Sessions records
Lic regs (for both public houses and beer shops): Wigan PS County Div, from *c.*1903; Leigh PS, Borough and County Div *c.*1900-1959s.
Lic regs (separate for victuallers and beer houses): Wigan PS, Borough Div from *c.*1890s.
Court registers: Wigan PS, Borough Div. from 1916; Wigan PS, County Div from 1920s; Leigh PS, Borough Div. from 1903; Leigh PS, County Div. from 1880.
Plans of licensed premises: Wigan PS, unsorted.

Greater Manchester Police Museum,
Newton Street, Manchester M1 1ES.
Tel. 0161 856 3287. Prior appointment essential.

'File D5 Licensing' - location code for where all archives relating to Licensing (for Manchester area) are stored (also Gambling, Gaming and Pawnbrokers). They are of varied nature and incomplete. No index; no detailed cataloguing. Include some registrations of licensed premises.

Merseyside Police Museum, *Publicity Department, Police HQ, Canning Place, Liverpool L69 1JD.*

Register of public houses, Index 'G' Division 1903.

LEICESTERSHIRE

Boroughs which were their own licensing authority: Leicester.
Licensing Divisions post-1828:
Ashby de la Zouch, East Norton, Leicester, Loughborough, Lutterworth, Market Bosworth, Market Harborough, Melton Belvoir, County of Rutland.

National records (see pages 6-8)

Letters Patent (1554-71): Leicester.
Vintners' fines (1569-72): None.
Victuallers' (Lenten) Recognizances (1572-1634).
Raleigh Wine Licences (1582-7, 1594-5).
Mompesson Licences (1620): Leicester, Melton Mowbray, Mountsorrel.
Coventry Wine Licences (1626-39): Ashby de la Zouch, Hinckley, Loughborough, Leicester, Melton Mowbray.
Wine Licences: Pipe Office (1670-1756).

The Record Office for Leicestershire, Leicester
and Rutland, Wigston Magna.

1552-1828: Inns and Alehouses

Quarter Sessions records
Original recogs, one only 1825; Victuallers' regs 1753-1827.

Borough records
Victuallers' recognizances 1566-72, 1649-62 (gaps), 1681-85, 1710-13, 1716-47.

1828 on: Inns, Public Houses and Beer Shops

Quarter Sessions records
Paper re applications for new lics or transfers, petitions for and against, lic plans etc, 1933, 1936-7.
Lic Ctee mins 1874-1932; Mins for 1872-4 found in general order books; Regs of summary convictions of licensed victuallers and beer sellers 1842-1915.

Petty Sessions records
Ashby de la Zouch. Lic regs 1842-1966.
East Norton. Lic regs 1887-1941.
Hinckley. Lic regs 1899-1965
Leicester (Borough), Lic regss c1877-1955, 1958-65, 1985-87;
Reg of protection roders for on & off lics. 1958-65.
Leicestershire County. Lic regs 1878-1960s, 1983-88.
Louchborough. Lic regs 1872-1960.
Lutterworth. Lic regs 1907-1947, 1983-88.
Melton & Belvoir. Lic regs 1911-62.

Deposited records
PH plans, Ashby Lic. District 19th century to *c.*1928.

LINCOLNSHIRE

Boroughs which were their own licensing authority:
Boston, Grantham, Lincoln, Louth, Stamford.
Licensing Districts post-1828:
Bradley Haverstoe, Caistor, Epworth, Lincoln
North, Louth, Sleaford, Spilsby, Wragby.

National records (see pages 6-8)

Letters Patent (1554-71): Bourne, Folkingham,
Grantham, Lincoln, Stamford.
Vintners' fines (1569-72): Caister, Donnington,
Gainsborough, Grantham, Horncastle, Lincoln,
Louth, Sleaford, Spalding.
Victuallers' (Lenten) Recognizances (1572-1634).
Raleigh Wine Licences (1582-6, 1591-7, 1601-2).
Mompesson Licences (1620): Boston, Bourne,
Coningsby, Horncastle, Kirton in Holland, 'Vale of
Linn' (Lincoln?), Skirbeck, (New) Sleaford,
Spalding, Swineshead, Whaplode.
Coventry Wine Licences (1626-39): Alford, Ancaster,
Bolingbroke, Boston, Burgh, Burton, Burwell,
Caistor, Crowle, Market Deeping, Durrington and
Crowland, Fleet, Gainsborough, Glandford Bridge,
Grantham, Horncastle, Lincoln, Louth, Market
Raisin, Sleaford, Spalding, Tattershall and
Coningsby, Wragby.
Wine Licences: Pipe Office (1670-1756).
Military Survey 1756 (see page 11). Granthan
Collection, various districts: places, names of
victuallers and signs, numbers of beds and
stabling [WO 30/49, ff.46-62].

Lincolnshire Archives, *Lincoln.*

1552-1828: Inns and Alehouses

*Quarter Sessions records for the Counties of
Holland, Kesteven and Lindsey*
Holland: Regs of alehouse recogs, Elloe and Kirton
and Skirbeck Wapentakes 1725-27, 1755-63; Lists
of recogs, Elloe Wapentake 1785, 1787-8.
Kesteven: Regs of lics 1678, 1684-1737 (with gaps),
1784-1812, 1825-62; Recogs 1735-56, 1827.
Lindsey: Reg of recogs 1632-38; Recogs 1792,
1796-99, 1802-21, 1823-28; Lists of lics: Kirton div
1807, Epworth 1828; Testimonials for licence
applications 1824, 1827; Copy of QS orders 1807.

1828 on: Inns, Public Houses and Beer Shops

Quarter Sessions
Kesteven: Papers re licences 1844-65.

Petty Sessions
Boston. Lic regs 1935-54.
Bradley Haverstoe: Licensed premises reg 1880-
1900, 1903-29.
Caistor: Lic regs 1890-1915.
Epworth. Applications for lics 1950-66.
    West Manley area, reg of lics 1872-99.
Elloe (Spalding, Long Sutton, Holbeach). Lic regs
1911-75.

Gainsborough. Lic regs 1872-1959.
Horncastle. Lic regs. 1875-1944.
Lincoln City. Lic regs 1872-1962.
Lincoln North: lics reg 1872-1901, 1908-56; Certs of
lics, and some JPs' orders 1833-57; Lic papers
1833-1854; Applications for beer house lics 1869.
Louth: Louth Borough, reg of lics 1890-1959; South
Lindsey, reg of lics 1903-1959.
Sleaford: List of lics *c*.1833-41.
Spilsby: Reg of alehouses 1896-1901; Reg of beer
and wine etc lics 1882-1901.
Wragby: Reg of lics 1880-1960.

Boston Borough Council Offices.

1552-1828: Inns and Alehouses

Boston Borough Sessions records
Reg of recogs 1817-26; QS mins contain recogs,
1732-56, 1780-94; Lists of licensees 1784-1855;
Applications 1814-84.

1828 on: Inns, Public Houses and Beer Shops

Boston Borough Sessions records (see also above)
Lists of renewals 1870-76; Appeals against alehouse
convictions 1859-1910; Petitions (concerning
licensing hours etc) 1825-89.

North East Lincolnshire Archives, *Grimsby.*

1552-1828: Inns and Alehouses

Grimsby Borough records
Alehouse bonds (recognizances) 1587-92.

1828 on: Inns, Public Houses and Beer Shops

Magistrates' Courts records
Grimsby Borough: Regs of lics 1889-1960; Reg of
lics referred 1909-33; Reg of lics extinguished
1909-35.
Registers of licences: Grimsby County 1930-71;
Barton-on-Humber 1932-74; Brigg 1903-74;
Scunthorpe 1949-67.

LONDON

National records (see pages 6-8)

Letters Patent (1554-71): City of London (suburbs),
see under Middlesex; otherwise none.
Vintners' fines (1569-72): None.
Raleigh Wine Licences (1583-1602): None.
Victuallers' (Lenten) Recognizances (1593-1641).
Mompesson Licences (1620): None.
Coventry Wine Licences (1626).
Wine Duty Farmers (1638-40). see right.
Wine Licences: Pipe Office (1670-1756).

London continued

1552-1828: Inns and Alehouses

Victuallers' licences (returns of those approved for
licensing for ensuing year) for each ward 1683 to
c.1750, a few at later dates. The returns also
include some petitions, certificates of good
character, and licences.

City freedom admission papers, from 1681.

Return of taverns and other papers re victuallers
1626-86 includes a return of taverns, 1663 [Alchin
Box H/103 no 11].

Sessions minutes and files may include some
general orders re licensing.

Sessions books: Orders of Quarter Sessions.

1828 on: Inns, Public Houses and Beer Shops

City Freedom admission papers; after 1853 licensed
victuallers not obliged to take up City Freedom.

Guildhall Justices' Room: Special Sessions Books
1858-1936, re new and discontinued lics.

Guildhall Justices' Room: Regs of lic'd victuallers
1873 onwards, include on and off licences.

Lic Ctee records: Notes on Views 1934-49; Reports
to Ctee re Surveyor's approval plans 1965-82 (30
year closure).

Surveyor's approval plans for new lics and
alterations 1890s-1982 (30 year closure).

Guildhall Library (Manuscripts Section),
Aldermanbury, London.

1552-1828: Inns and Alehouses

Lists of victuallers' bonds (recogs) St. Anne's
Blackfriars 1724-37 [Ms.7888]; Petitions, lists and
other papers re licensed victuallers, Bridge Ward
Within 1807-1815 [Mss.5788, 8576].

Society of Licensed Victuallers, records, 1794-1925
[Ms 21439-57].

1828 on: Inns, Public Houses and Beer Shops

Parish and Ward records

Petitions, notices and other papers re licensing,
St. Dionis Backchurch, St. Faith under St. Paul,
Portsoken Ward c.1831-72 [Ms.3494].

Bread Street Ward. Incl. lists of licensed victuallers
c.1857-c1891 [Ms 1238].

Licences for other activities

Vintners' Company records

Charters, letters patent, ordinances, bye-laws, corres
etc concerning the Vintners' privilege to retail wine
without individual licences 1553-1856.

Ledgers and accounts kept by Vintners' Company as
Receivers of the Wine Licences (wine duty
farmers) 1638-40 [Mss.15353-5].

Goldsmiths' Company records

Victualling licences issued to tenants, Goldsmiths'
Company 1779 [formerly Ms.8744, now returned to
the Goldsmiths' Company].

MIDDLESEX

Licensing Divisions

Inner London Divisions (County of London from
1889) 1872-1954:

Blackheath (Kent), Finsbury, Hampstead, Holborn,
Kensington, Newington, Paddington,
St. Marylebone, St. Pancras, Stoke Newington,
Tower, Wandsworth (Surrey), Westminster.

Middlesex Divisions, 1869-1973:

Brentford, Edmonton, Gore, Highgate, South
Mimms, Spelthorne, Uxbridge, Willesden.

National records *(see pages 6-8)*

Letters Patent (1554-71): City of London (suburbs),
City of Westminster, Brentford, Hoggsden(?),
Hounslow, Norton Folley(?), St. Giles, St.
Katherine's, Smithfield, Tottenham, Uxbridge.

Vintners' fines (1569-72): None.

Victuallers' (Lenten) Recognizances (1572-1634).

Raleigh Wine Licences (1596-7).

Mompesson Licences (1620): Acton, Bedfont,
Bethnal Green, Brentford, Chelsea, Drury Lane,
Edgware, Enfield, Finsbury, Fulham, Goswell
Street, Grays Inn Lane, Hackney, Harrow on the
Hill, 'Harts Horne Lane', Holborn, Islington,
Kensington, Knightsbridge, South Mimms,
Northcott(?), Old Cross Street, Pinner, Potters Bar,
Ruislip, St. Giles, St. John Street, St. Martin's (in
the Fields), 'Shepp Yard', Staines, Stepney,
Westminster, Whitechapel.

Coventry Wine Licences (1626-39): Acton, Bedfont,
Brentford, Chelsea, Cowcrosse, Clerkenwell,
Grays Inn Lane, Hackney, Hampstead, Hayes,
Highgate, Hillingdon, Holborn, Holloway Street,
Hornsey, Hounslow, Isleworth, Islington,
Kensington, Knightsbridge, Limehouse, Longford,
South Mimms, Newington, Pinner, Poplar,
Ratcliffe, St Giles in the Fields, St John Street, St
Martin in the Fields, Staines, Stanwell, Strand,
Tottenham Street, Tuttle Street, Turnbull Street,
Whetstone, Whitechapel.

Wine Licences: Pipe Office (1670-1756).

London Metropolitan Archives

1552-1828: Inns and Alehouses

Middlesex Quarter Sessions records

Recognizance Roll 1552 records details of alehouse
recognizances for limited number of parishes.

Book of Informations contains presentments re
alehouse keepers and other traders 1624-37.

Sessions registers from 1608-1667, and sessions
books from 1639-1687, contain some references
to recognizances, presentments etc.

Sessions Books and Orders of Court, 1716-1751:
these contain many references to licensing
alehouse keepers and brandy sellers and the
problems of licensing retail of spirits.

Victuallers' regs, Mins of of recogs 1716-1752, with
gaps.

Middlesex: *London Metropolitan Archives* contd

Original recognizances 1754-1826 with gaps.
Registers for each licensing district 1758-1829.
Certificates of good character 1788-1826, with gaps.
Constables' returns of sellers of brandy and
victuallers 1743-1852, with gaps.
Fines and convictions 1824.

Westminster Quarter Sessions
Regs 1687-1753 (gaps), Mins of recogs 1712-53,
(gaps); Regs for each lic district 1793-1813 (gaps);
Original recogs 1689-1828 (gaps).
Constables' returns for victuallers and brandy sellers
1711, 1712, 1726, 1731, 1737, 1747.

1828 on: Inns, Public Houses and Beer Shops

Quarter Sessions records
Licensing Committee records: Mins contain lists of
names of applicants and types of lics 1886-1901;
Papers passed on from divisional licensing
sessions incl notices of intention to apply for lic,
surveyors' reports, plans, police reports. and
petitions from local residents 1878-1888.
Rating certificates for prospective beer shops,
St. James Westminster 1850-61, 1862-67.

Petty Sessional Licensing records
Regs of lics for the separate Licensing Divisions.
   These usually record the names of applicants,
   addresses and signs:
Finsbury Div 1851, 1854, 1875-1955; Hampstead
Div 1922-53; Holborn Div 1873-1956; Kensington
Div 1873-1948; Newington Div 1869-1953;
St. Pancras Div 1886-1956; Stoke Newington Div
1890-1956 ; Wandsworth Div 1877-1911 ;
Edmonton Div 1869-70; Gore Div 1873-1973;
Highgate Div 1876-1949; South Mimms 1872-
1938; Willesden Div 1873-1922.
Calendars of licences: Newington Div 1774-1915.
Regs of transfers of lics: Wandsworth Div 1923-61.

Other licensing activities
Quarter Sessions records
Music and dancing Lics 1752, 1763-1781, 1823,
1844, 1880-81 (gaps); Lists of lics (printed) issued
previous year with notes re renewals 1849, 1858-
1888; Police reports concerning licensees who
sold spirits without licences 1862-73 (gaps); JPs'
and police reports listing names of applicants and
whether licensed as public houses etc, 1863-73.

Greater London History Library (L.M.A.)
---

*Middlesex County Records: Calendar of Sessions
   Books and Orders*, 12 vols, 1714-1751. Ts.
*Calendar to a Volume entitled 'Brentford Journal'
   being a Record of the Proceedings at Petty
   Sessions held at Brentford, 1651-1714.* Ts.
Both indexed: subjects, places and personal names.

Middlesex continued

City of Westminster Archives Centre,
10 St. Ann's Street, London SW1P 2XR.

1552-1828: Inns and Alehouses

Petty Sessions records
St. Anne, Soho: PS mins incl lics 1749-92; Regs of
   lic'd victuallers 1754-1813;
St. James, Piccadilly: Mins incl lics 1765-96.
St. Margaret and St. John, Westminster: Mins 1707-
   1780, 1801.
St. Marylebone: Regs of alehouse lics 1822-28.

1828 on: Inns, Public Houses and Beer Shops

Petty and Special Sessions records
St. James, Piccadilly: Regs of lics 1856-64.
St. James Div (including St. Anne): Mins, incl lics
   1825-1955; Regs of full and beer lics 1828-1956;
   Lic transfers 1832-1961 (gaps); Regs of conviction
   1837-1920.
Strand Div: Mins, incl beer licences 1853-87; Regs of
   full and beer lics 1873-1959; Lic ctee mins 1888-
   1956.
St. Margaret's Div: Regs of full and of beer lics and
   transfers 1921-57; Lic ctee mins 1927-56.
Hanover Square Div:Reg of lics 1903-57; Lic ctee
   mins 1902-56.
Marylebone Div: Regs of lics 1829-1941 [earlier regs
   at GLRO]; Mins of JPs of St. Marylebone Division,
   eight volumes, 1822-1932; Agenda book of JPs
   1923-26.
Westminster Div (all areas): Regs of lic transfers
   1961-72; Lic ctee mins 1959-62.
Ordnance Survey map marked with licensed
   premises c.1950.

Other licensing activities
From 1846 St. Marylebone regs include lics for
billiards and other games.

Camden Archives and Local Studies Library,
Holborn Library.

Transcripts of annual returns of St. Pancras lic'd
victuallers, 1721-1802 (from GLRO holdings).

Stratford Library (London Borough of Newham).

West Ham and East Ham etc., see under Essex.

Wandsworth Library.

See under Surrey.

No relevant records held by *Battersea Library, Ealing
Local History Library, Hackney Archives
Department, Hammersmith and Fulham Archives
Department, Islington Central Library, Kensington
and Chelsea (Local Studies) Central Library.*

Monmouthshire - see with *Wales*, page 56.

NORFOLK

Boroughs known to be own licensing authority:
Norwich, Great Yarmouth, King's Lynn, Thetford.
Licensing divisions set up after 1828:
Blofield and Walsham, Clackclose, Diss, Flegg,
East and West, Earsham, Erpingham, North
Erpingham, South Eynsford, Freebridge Lynn,
Gallow, North Greenhoe, South Greenhoe,
Grimshoe, Holt, King's Lynn, Mitford and
Launditch, Norwich, Smithdon and Brothercross,
Taverham, Thetford, Tunstead and Happing,
Wayland.

National records (see pages 6-8)

Letters Patent (1554-71):
Attleborough, Brodisham(?), Harleston Market(?),
King's Lynn, Norwich, Watton.
Vintners' fines (1569-72): Attleborough, Aylsham,
Burnham Ulph, Buxton, Great Yarmouth, Higham,
Kings Lynn, Litcham, Norwich, Sopham, Thetford,
Walsingham.
Victuallers' (Lenten) Recognizances (1572-1634).
Raleigh Wine Licences (1596-7).
Mompesson Licences (1620): Attleborough,
Aylsham, Bale, Beeston, Binham, Bintree,
Bradfield, Brancaster, Bringham, Briningham, New
and Old Buckenham, Bunwell, Burnham, Buxton,
Castle Acre, Caston, Caston Woodrowe, Catton,
Colby, Corpusty, South Creake, Deopham, East
and West Dereham, Diss, Downham Market,
Drayton, Eaton, (North) Ellingham, Fakenham,
Felmingham, Foulden, Foulsham, Garboldisham,
Garveston, Gillingham, Guist, Hackford, Hainford,
Hargham, East Harling, Hatchston(?), Hempnall,
Hellesdon, Hethersett, Hevingham, Hickling,
Hilborough, Hindolveston, Hindringham, Hingham,
Hockham, Holme, Holt, Houghton, Jarmans
Bridge, Kenninghall, Kettleston, Kings Lynn,
Langham, West Lexham, Loddon, North Lopham,
Lyng, Marsham, Mattishall, Moreley, Mulbarton,
Neateshead, Newton Flotman, Norwich, Rockland,
East Rudham, Saham Toney, St. Faiths,
Saxthorpe, Sculthorpe, Seachey(?), Sharrington,
Sheringham, Shropham, (Great) Snoring,
Sparham, Stibbard, Stradishall(?), Suyterby(?),
Swainsthorpe, Swanton Abbot, Swanton Morley,
Swanton Novers, Thetford, Thornham, Thursford,
Trowse, Trunch, Twyford, Ulterton(?), North and
South Walsham, Great and Little Walsingham,
Warham, Winchingham(?), Winfarthing, Wiveton,
Woodrowe(?), Wymondham.
Coventry Wine Licences (1626-39): Acle,
Attleborough, Bawdeswell, Burnham Westgate,
Diss, Foulsham, Kings Lynn, Old Lynn and Rising,
Norwich, Scole, Setchey, Swafffham, Yarmouth.
Wine Licences: Pipe Office (1670-1756).

Norfolk Record Office, *Norwich.*

1552-1828: Inns and Alehouses

County Quarter Sessions records
Alehouse keepers' recog rolls: 1634; 1648-73, 1808;
Freebridge Marshland Hundred, 1649 and
Clackclose Hundred, 1653; Alehouse keepers'
recog reg, 1789-99, with index by parish.

Borough Records

Norwich City Quarter Sessions records
Innkeepers and Tipplers Book, 1587-1597; Original
alehouse keepers' recognizances 1760-1807 with
transcript and index; Pre-1760 recognizances are
entered in Sessions minute books.
City Lease Books B-D, 1665-1828, include copies of
wine licences [NCR Case 22d].

Norwich Cathedral Precinct QS records
Original alehouse keepers' recognizances 1801-28.

Great Yarmouth Borough Quarter Sessions records
Alehouse keepers' recognizance rolls 1683, 1687.
List of innkeepers naming inns and brewers 1819.

King's Lynn Borough Quarter Sessions records
[Held by Borough Council of King's Lynn and West
Norfolk; access to be arranged by appointment
through Norfolk Record Office.]
List of alehouse keepers' recogs 1629-30, 1639.

Thetford Borough Quarter Sessions records
[Held by Thetford Town Council; list available in
Record Office.]
Licensing sessions mins 1682-86; Alehouse
keepers' recogs 1571-84 (gaps), 1620-29.
Petty Sessions records
King's Lynn PS alehouse lic records 1794-1808.

1828 on: Inns, Public Houses and Beer Shops

County records
Norfolk County Council Lic Ctee mins 1905-74.

Petty Sessions records
(Closed to public inspection for 30 years)
Registers of licences: Blofield and Walsingham 1872-
1973; Clackclose 1917-49; Diss 1928-69; Earsham
1933-67; Erpingham, North 1872-1902, 1908-35,
1937-81; Erpingham, South 1925-75; Eynsford
1878 1970 [NB 1878-1927 are fragile and cannot
be consulted]; Flegg, East and West 1903-1973;
Freebridge Lynn 1950-71; Freebridge Marshland
1936-60; Gallow 1905-1975; Greenhoe, North
1906-74; Greenhoe, South 1926-69; Grimshoe
(merged with Thetford 1954) 1926-54; Holt 1878-
1956, 1958-62; King's Lynn 1872-1965; Mitford and
Launditch 1901-1975; Norwich 1867-1982;
Smithdon and Brothercross 1949-65; Taverham
1872-1887, 1903-73; Thetford (merged with
Grimshoe in 1954 to form Thetford and Grimshoe)
1922-66; Tunstead and Happing 1928-1980;
Wayland 1937-69; Yarmouth, Great 1949-81.

Norfolk: *Norfolk Record Office*, continued

Petty Sessions records continued

Registers of transfer of licences: Erpingham, South: Reg of appointments of parish officers and transfer of lics 1893-1929; Gallow: Mins incl transfers of alehouse lics 1859-74; Norwich: Regs of applications and transfers of all lics and of applications for structural alterations 1894-1972.

Plans of proposed alterations to public houses deposited with licensing justices Norwich 1948-1957.

Licensing Compensation Authorities' records: Norwich Lic. Comp. Auth. mins 1905-36; agreements 1929-39, and other papers 1915-72; Yarmouth, Great, Lic. Comp. Auth. mins and correspondence, 1966-74.

Other licences

Borough records
Norwich Mayor's Court Book, No 7, 1555-62 has entries for licensing wine retailers.
Three wine licences, 1737, 1747, 1751.
Beer brewers trade bye-laws 1668.

Petty Sessions records
Music and dancing regs: Erpingham, North 1972-1980; Flegg, East and West 1949-74; Holt 1960-1975, also copy of Sunday music lics 1961-66; King's Lynn 1892-1956; Norwich 1910-82; Tunstead and Happing 1975-80; Yarmouth, Great 1948-80, also register of lics (under Sunday Entertainment Act of 1932) 1957-74.
Billiards licences registers: Norwich 1869-1966.

NORTHAMPTONSHIRE

Licensing Districts to 1790 are the Hundred, from 1790 by licensing divisions: Daventry, Kettering, Northampton (not the borough), Oundle, Thorpe Mandeville (covering south of the county), and Towcester.

National Records (see pages 6-8)

Letters Patent (1554-71): Northampton, Stamford (Baron), Stilton, Wellingborough.
Vintners' fines (1569-72): Daventry, Northampton, Towcester.
Victuallers' (Lenten) Recognizances (1572-1634).
Raleigh Wine Licences (1585-6).
Mompesson Licences (1620): Brixworth, Collyweston, Croughton, Daventry, Deene, Denford, Gretton, Kelmarsh, Kings Cliffe, Middleton Cheney, Stamford Baron, Towcester, Wappenham, Weedon Beck, Wellingborough.
Coventry Wine Licences (1626-39): Grafton Regis, Higham Ferrers, Kilsby, Northampton, Oundle, Peterborough, Weedon Bec, 'Weldon'.
Wine Licences: Pipe Office (1670-1756).

Northamptonshire continued

Northamptonshire Record Office, Northampton.

1552-1828: Inns and Alehouses

Family papers
The Finch Hatton collection contains a series of early licensing records:
1615. Individual recogs [FH 1077-1116];
1630. Rules for licensing [FH 18];
1630. Recog file for whole county except Soke of Peterborough and boroughs [FH 2962];
1637. Recogs for Spelhoe, Wymersley and Nobottle Hundreds [FH 120].
1690. Recogs. for Willibrook Hundred [293/7].
1690-1706. Recogs for Corby Hundred [FH 293].

Quarter Sessions records
1661-1692. Sessions Rolls contain sheets of recogs, for Hundreds a follows. *Asterisk = faded.
Brackley (Borough). 1692 (also 1673-74?).
Cleyley. 1661, 1665, 1673-74.
Corby. 1673-74, 1682 (damaged). See also above.
Fawsley. 1673-74.
Guilsborough. 1662*, 1673-74.
Hamfordshoe. 1666, 1668*, 1669, 1673-74, 1681.
Higham Ferrers. 1666, 1669, 1673-74, 1681.
Huxloe. 1673-74, 1681.
Nassaburgh [Soke of Peterborough]. The Soke has its own series of QS records.
Navisford. 1661, 1673-74.
Nobottle Grove. 1661, 1665, 1673-74.
Green's Norton. 1661, 1662, 1666, 1673-74.
Orlingbury. 1669, 1673-74, 1681.
Polebrook. 1661, 1673-74.
Rothwell. 1673-74, 1681, 1682.
Spelhoe. 1661, 1662*, 1665, 1673-74.
King's Sutton. 1661, 1662, 1666, 1673-74.
Towcester. 1661, 1662*, 1665, 1763-74.
Chipping Warden. 1661, 1662, 1665, 1666, 1673-74.
Wellingborough [not a Hd?]. 1669.
Willybrook. 1661, 1673-74, 1681.
Wymersley. 1661, 1665, 1673-74.

Rolls for **1673** and **1674** and Original recognizances **1737-1828** cover whole county except Soke and Northampton. From 1737 they are by Division rather than Hundred - see left.

Borough records:
Daventry. Recogs 1782-98.
Higham Ferrers. Recogs 1757-63, 1773-80.
Northampton. Assembly books record orders re alehouses, 1553-17th century. Index 1553-1629..

Soke of Peterborough [Nassaburgh Hd.]. The Soke has its own series of QS records.

1828 on: Inns, Public Houses and Beer Shops

Quarter Sessions records
Liquor Lic Ctee mins 1872-1900, 1905-61; corres 1872-1907.
Compensation Authority: Ledger 1904-28; Mins Northampton Borough 1906-60; financial statements 1905-20.

Northamptonshire: *Northants R.O.* continued

Petty Sessions records
Brackley Div: Returns 1878-1948; Regs 1869-1901, 1903-62.
Daventry Div: Regs 1890-1900; Police regs 1891-1973.
Higham Ferrers Div: Reg 1903-24.
Kettering Div: Lic ctee 1830-34; Regs 1872-1953; Charge sheets 1854-58, 1863-78.
Little Bowden Div: Corres 1880-81; Regs 1872-93, 1903, 1911-48.
Northampton Borough Div: Police regs 1888-1967; Borough regs on/off and victuallers 1903-50; Reg of plans of licensed houses 1903-05, and planning applications 1903-36.
Oundle Div: Regs 1928-67.
Peterborough Div: Regs 1878-82, 1886-89, Files 1923, 1933-63.
Thrapston Div: Returns 1902; Regs 1913-73.
Towcester Div: Mins 1879-87; Transfers of lics 1885-1886.
Wellingborough Div: Regs 1891-1970.

Northamptonshire Police Archives,
Police HQ, Wootton Hall, Northampton NN4 0JQ.

Chief Constable's licensing reports, Northampton Borough Police, 4 vols., 1901-1965.

NORTHUMBERLAND

Boroughs which were their own licensing authority:
Newcastle upon Tyne.
Licensing Districts post-1828:
Alnwick, Bamburgh, Bedlingtonshire, Bellingham, Berwick, East Castle Ward, East Coquetdale, Norham and Islandshire, North Coquetdale, Tindale, Newcastle upon Tyne.

National Records (see pages 6-8)

Letters Patent (1554-71): Newcastle.
Vintners' fines (1569-72): None.
Victuallers' (Lenten) Recognizances (1572-1634).
Raleigh Wine Licences (1596-7).
Mompesson Licences (1620): None.
Coventry Wine Licences (1626-39): Morpeth, Newcastle upon Tyne, North Shields.
Wine Licences: Pipe Office (1670-1756).

Northumberland Collections Service,
Ashington.

1552-1828: Inns and Alehouses

Quarter Sessions records
Presentments for disorderly houses 1698-99; Suppression of disorderly alehouses, 1700; Ban to prevent reopening of alehouse 1698; General licensing orders, 1723; Stricter regulation for granting licences, 1747.
Register of alehouse recognizances 1822-26; typed transcript.

Northumberland: *Collections Service* contd.

Delaval Family papers
Names of JP's taking bonds for alehouse keepers in several wards, 1618 [IDE7/56]; 20 recogs, 1618 [IDE7/59, IDE7/61]; List of certified alehouses 1618 [IDE7/60]; Order to sheriff and bailiffs of Tynedale Ward to proceed against unlicensed alehouse keepers, 1619 [IDE7/69]; Copy of alehouse lics *c.*1618 [IDE7/75+76].

1828 on: Inns, Public Houses and Beer Shops

Quarter Sessions records
Order books: Petition against increase in number of alehouse lics, 1839; PS licensing alehouses, 1848.

Other County records
Mins of licensing ctee, 1905-35; Applications for confirmation of lics 1890-1950; List of lics laid before ctee 1875-1904; Statement of lics referred to ctee 1905-69; Reg of lics referred and subsequent proceedings 1905-77; Corres etc 1906-45.

Petty Sessions records
Bedlington Div: Reg of lics 1872-1970.
Bellingham Div: Reg of lics 1874-99.
Tindale Div: Lic reg 1948-*c.*1960.
North Coquetdale Div: Whittingham reg of lics 1922-1968.
East Coquetdale Div: Reg of lics 1911-37, 1944-62.
West Coquetdale Div: Reg of lics 1934-73.

Constabulary records
Newcastle: Regs of beer houses *c.*1890-1967; list of licensed houses, Alnwick Division 1910-46.

Licences for other activities
Petty Sessions records
Regs of music and dancing lics: Bedlington Div, 1925-73; East Castle Ward Div 1925-52; Tindale Div 1915-67.

Berwick-upon-Tweed Record Office.

1552-1828: Inns and Alehouses

Borough Records
Berwick Bailiff's court book contains presentments for keeping alehouses, 1568-1603.
Brewers licensing book 1685-*c.*1710.
Quarter Sessions order book contains presentments for brewing without licence, 1694-1727, annual lists of recognizances 1694-1781.
Original recognizances 1767-1779, 1810-1822.

1828 on: Inns, Public Houses and Beer Shops
Petty Sessions records
Berwick Div: Mins of JPs' meeting incl lic ctee meetings 1921-35; Regs of alehouse lics 1903-46.
Norham and Islandshire Div: Reg of alehouse lics 1913-61.
Bamburgh Div: Reg of lics 1913-35.

Other licences
Petty Sessions records
Regs of music and dancing lics: Berwick Div 1914-1936.

Northumberland continued

> ### Tyne & Wear Archives Service,
> *Newcastle upon Tyne.*

1552-1828: Inns and Aehouses

Newcastle Quarter Sessions records
Registers of alehouse recognizances 1822-28.

1828 on: Inns, Public Houses and Beer Shops

Newcastle Quarter Sessions records
Accounts for fines paid as a result of breach of
conditions of alehouse recognizances 1828-29.

Petty Sessions records
East Cstle Ward: alcohol lics reg 1872-1960.
Newcastle: Publicans' lics regs 1872-1965; Beer,
wine and spirit lics regs 1872-1972; Licensing
minutes 1873-1945.
North Tyneside (formerly Tynemouth Borough): Lic
regs for publicans, beerhouses, on and off lics,
sale of beer, wines and spirits 1925-65; Plans of
PHs submitted to licensing JPs c.1903-74.
Wallsend Borough PS Div: Wine and spirit lics regs
1910-72.
West Castle Ward PS: Lic regs 1872-1960; Lic plans
1874-1948.

Police records
Newcastle upon Tyne Borough Constabulary:
Registers of licensed premises 1869-1966.

Other licences
Music and dancing: East Castle Ward 1925-53;
Newcastle 1931-64; North Tyneside 1933-82;
Wallsend 1925-74.

NOTTINGHAMSHIRE

Boroughs known to be own licensing authority:
Nottingham, Newark.

> ### National Records (see pages 6-8)

Letters Patent (1554-71): Mansfield, Newark,
Nottingham.
Vintners' fines (1569-72): Nottingham, Tuxford.
Victuallers' (Lenten) Recognizances (1572-1634).
Raleigh Wine Licences (1596-7).
Mompesson Licences (1620): None.
Coventry Wine Licences (1626-39): Newark,
Nottingham, Worksop.
Wine Licences: Pipe Office (1670-1756).

> ### Nottinghamshire Archives, Nottingham.

1552-1828: Inns and Alehouses

Quarter Sessions records
Lists of alehouse keepers, 1675, parts of Hundreds
of Broxtowe and Thurgarton.
County victuallers' registers, 1809-1827.

Nottinghamshire: *Nottinghamshire Archives* ctd.

Borough records
Nottingham, victuallers' registers 1758-61, 1756-69.
Published: *Nottingham Alehouse Recognizances
1756-69.* Notts FHS Record Soc. **94** (1994).

1828 on: Inns, Public Houses and Beer Shops

Quarter Sessions records
County lic ctee mins 1873-1951; Confirming and
compensation ctee mins 1952-73.

*Petty sessions records or Magistrates' Courts
records* (some at present unlisted, subject to
access restrictions)
Mansfield. Registers of alehouses and beerhouses:
Mansfield Div 1873-1950; Mansfield Borough
1914-1950; Lic regs c1967-2005; Individual lic files
and places C20; Betting and gaming regs c1960-
2007; Regs of clubs: Mansfield borough 1921-29;
div 1903-20, c1962-2004; Reg of premises
licensed for music, dancing etc: Mansfield Borough
1937-51; Mansfield Div 1895-1952.
Newark and Southwell. Registers of alehouses and
beerhouses: Newark Borough 1872-1926; Newark
Div 1872-1898; Lics regs: Newark 1898-1990;
Southwell 1903-90; Newark & Southwell 1984-
2004; Courts reg Newark div lic applications 1973-
1974; Clubs reg: Newark 1903-62; Southwell 1946-
1962; Newark & Southwell 1962-68; *Other
activities:* Betting & gaming regs 1962-98, 2006;
Bingo lics regs c1970-80; Reg of premises lic'd for
music, dancing etc: Newark Borough 1939-51.
Nottingham. Magistrates' meetings mins, ctee and
brewster sessions 1874-1890; Licensing Ctee
mins: Nottingham City 1891-1934, 1975-87, 1990-
1994, Bingham 1971-87; Justices lic mins 1962-
1987; Registers of alehouses and beerhouses:
Nottingham City, alehouses 1904-39; beerhouses
1916-39; Nottingham Div 1872-1949; Lic regs
1907-97; Compensation Authority mins, 1905-62,
1939-62, 1974-81; Court regs 1986-2005;
Nottingham Div. reg of lics 1949-73; lic
applications regs 1976-77, 1979-84; Individual lics
files and plans C20; Betting & gaming Lic Ctee mins
1959-93; permits and regs 1961-2005; Clubs reg
1947-62, Clubs reg (incl. Bingham) c1962-98;
Regs of clubs: Nottingham (city) 1947-62; (div)
1903-1962; Bingham div 1909-62; Reg of
premises licensed for music, dancing etc:
Nottingham City 1892-1939. General
correspondence, Nottingham 1904-1955;
Licensing plans, Nottingham 20th century.
Worksop and East Retford. Lic regs: Worksop
1873-1948; Worksop (Borough & County Div)
1934-67; East Retford (Borough Div) 1873-79,
1892-1901, 1903-67; East Retford (County Div)
1902-67; Worksop & East Retford 1999-2005; Lic
ctee mins: Worksop 1990-98, East Retford 1990-
2002; Worksop & East Retford 1989-1994;
Justices lic mins c1968-2205; Individual lic files &
plans C20; Betting & gaming regs. c1955-2008;
Music & dancing lics regs: Worksop 1969-74;

Nottinghamshire: *Nottinghamshire Archives* ctd.
Worksop and East Retford continued

Worksop annual lic meeting/transfer session mins 1935-66; betting lic ctee mins 1961-77; music and dancing lics reg 1934-68; Regs of clubs: Retford Borough 1962-73; Worksop div 1939-62; Worksop & Retford c1963-2005.

OXFORDSHIRE

Boroughs which were their own licensing authority:
Oxford (note Oxford University also had licensing rights), Banbury, Chipping Norton, Henley.
Licensing Districts post-1828:
Bullingdon, Henley Borough, Henley, Oxford City, Watlington.

National Records (see pages 6-8)

Letters Patent (1554-71): Banbury, Bicester, Henley, Oxford.
Vintners' fines (1569-72): Burford, Dorchester, Witney.
Victuallers' (Lenten) Recognizances (1572-1634).
Raleigh Wine Licences (1582-1602): None.
Mompesson Licences (1620): Chipping Norton, Enstone, Henley, Islip, Kirtlington, Oxford, Sandford (on Thames), Thame.
Coventry Wine Licences (1626-39): Benson, Burford, Chipping Norton, Deddington, Enstone, Henley, Islip, Nettlebed, Oxford, Tetsworth, Thame, Woodstock.
Wine Licences: Pipe Office (1670-1756).

Oxfordshire Record Office, Cowley, Oxford.

1552-1828: Inns and Alehouses

Quarter Sessions
Sessions Rolls 1687-1830 contain some references to alehouse licensing. Calendar and index on DVD published by Oxfordshire FHS (www.ofhs.org.uk>).
Sessions Minute Books 1688-1768 also contain references: consult the transcript with index under 'alehouses' and 'clerk of the peace'.
There are also references to spirit licences, and general orders and reports.
Victuallers' regs 1753-1822 [QSD.V.1-4]. 1769 pub'd.
Certificates of good character.

Borough records
Banbury: Wine licences 1676-94 (see *Banbury Corporation Records: Tudor and Stuart*, Banbury HS **15**, 1977).
Chipping Norton: The records contain some victuallers' papers. 1769 published, see right.
Henley: A few references.
Woodstock: Portmouth Court act books 1604-35, 1666-1676, 1691-1766; Council minute books 1767-1844; 1769 vic lics published, see right..

Oxford City Quarter Sessions records
Licences 1579-1759; for other records researchers should consult the Catalogue to the City QS.

Oxfordshire: *Oxfordshire Record Office* continued

1828 on: Inns, Public Houses and Beer Shops

Petty Sessions records
Bullingdon Div: Reg of lics 1911-72.
Henley Borough: Reg of lics 1887-1963; Papers on licensing, including objections, 1903-31.
Henley Div: Reg of lics 1882-1973; Loose papers on licences, including objections 1899-1911.
Oxford City: Reg of lics 1902-25.
Watlington Div: Reg of lics 1925-51.

Other licences
Music and dancing lics; Bullingdon Division 1955-1962, 1964-73.

Oxford University.

See *Register of the University of Oxford,* ed. Andrew Clark, vol. 2, Pt 1, Oxford Historical Society **10** (1887), pp. 322-27 for names of innkeepers and vintners, 1558-1662, and tavern keepers, 1567-1610, in Oxford, licensed by the University. Names of houses not given.

Thames Valley Police Museum, Police Training College, Sulhampstead, Reading.

Oxfordshire Constabulary
Register of public houses, Watlington.

Oxford City Police
Chief Constable's reports to the licensing ctee, 4 vols, 1898-1946.

Miscellaneous
Licensed houses, Banbury and Bloxham, 1905-1954.
Wootton North licences 1905-1953.
Borough of Banbury, licensed victuallers, c.1879-1954.

Publications: *Oxfordshire Licensed Victuallers 1769* [QSD.V.1], The Eureka Partnership, 2006.
V. Wood, *The Licensees ... of Banbury,* Oxon FHS; *The Licensees of Adderbury...,* Adderbury Hist Assn.

RUTLAND

National Records (see pages 6-8)

Letters Patent (1554-71): None.
Vintners' fines (1569-72): None.
Victuallers' (Lenten) Recognizances (1572-1634).
Raleigh Wine Licences (1582-3, 1584-5, 1586-7).
Mompesson Licences (1620): Great Casterton, Oakham, Uppingham.
Coventry Wine Licences (1626-39): Oakham.
Wine Licences: Pipe Office (1670-1756).

The Record Office for Leicestershire, Leicester and Rutland, Wigston Magna.

Rutland is listed as a licensing district, but no records held.

SHROPSHIRE

Boroughs known to be their own licensing authority: Bridgnorth, Ludlow, Shrewsbury.
Licensing Divisions post-1828:
Condover, Drayton and Whitchurch, Ellesmere, Ford, Newport, Oswestry Borough, Oswestry County, Pimhill, Pontesbury, Shifnal, and Wellington.

National Records (see pages 6-8)

Letters Patent (1554-71): Bridgnorth, Ludlow, Shrewsbury.
Vintners' fines (1569-72): Drayton, Oswestry, Shifnal, Wellington.
Victuallers' (Lenten) Recognizances (1572-1634).
Raleigh Wine Licences (1582-3).
Mompesson Licences (1620): Alvcley, Newport.
Coventry Wine Licences (1626-39): Bridgnorth, Newport, Shrewsbury, Church Stretton.
Wine Licences: Pipe Office (1670-1756).

Shropshire Archives, Shrewsbury.

1552-1828: Inns and Alehouses

Quarter Sessions records
Rolls include original recognizancess and lists of licensed victuallers etc 1696-1828.
Register of licensed alesellers 1613-31.
Registers of alehouse recognizancess 1753-1828.
List of licensed alehouses/victuallers: Pimhill Hundred 1782-1800; Drayton 1754.

Borough records
Bridgnorth: Alehouse recogs 1651-1688; Files and papers incl presentments 1634-1703; Names of persons breaking the assize 1669-70; Names of lic'd victuallers 1721, 1777, 1787-1789; Summons to cider retailer to appear 1722; Lists of victuallers entering into recogs with names of pubs, 1820-29; Certificates of good character 1823-24; QS rolls 1717-18, files and papers incl presentments 1700-1717, 1723, 1730-1828.
Ludlow. *Ludlow QS records:* Recog Books 1577-1617, 1685-99, 1742-1798; Recogs (in Order Book) 1707-41; Presentments 1701-46; Rolls/Files 1522, 1541-1828; *Ludlow Town Court records:* Recog Books 1562-1705, 1715.
Shrewsbury: Four books of ale sellers licences 1620-1737; Names of ale sellers 1690; Interrogatory as to ale selling 1594; Names of 68 innkeepers with pub names 1719-20; QS rolls contain references 1564-1828; Recogs to appear to answer charges of all sorts 1753-66.

Corbert of Longnor family papers
Petition of Shrewsbury innkeepers, c.1722-27

1828 on: Inns, Public houses and Beer Shops

Quarter Sessions records
Lic returns for county, 1891, 1896, 1901; Lic returns for Shrewsbury 1903; Licensing ctee mins 1905-1973; Compensation papers, 1906-35, 1940-41.

Petty Sessions records
Victuallers' registers: Condover Div 1872-3; Ellesmere Div 1942-60; Ford Div 1872-88; Pontesbury Div 1907-20; Oswestry County Div 1949; Pimhill Div 1902-54.
Licensing plans and maps, Condover Division.
Survey of lic'd prems Oswestry Borough, pre-1954.

Police records
Applications for summonses for public house and beer shop offences: Oswestry Div 1840-1941; Drayton and Whitchurch Div 1840-1941; Wellington, Newport 1893-1937; Clunbury, Condover and Ford Divs 1887-1936.

Other licences
Music and dancing lic regs: Oswestry Div, Oswestry Borough and Ellesmere Benches 1954-1983.

Wenlock Borough (c/o Wenlock Town Council).

Alehouse keepers' recogs and registers 1764-1851.

SOMERSET

Boroughs known to be their own licensing authority:
Bath.
Licensing Divisions, post-1828:
Bishops Lydeard, Bridgwater Borough, Crewkerne, Dunster, Glastonbury Borough, Wiveliscombe, Ilminster, Long Ashton, Taunton, Taunton Borough, Wells City, Williton, Yeovil Borough.

National Records (see pages 6-8)

Letters Patent (1554-71): Bruton, Congresbury, Dunster, Glastonbury, Ilminster, Milverton, Wells.
Vintners' fines (1569-72): Axbridge, Barrow, Bath, Bleadon, Bruton, Bridgwater, Chard, Combwick(?), Crewkerne, Crewkerne Pill, Dunster, Frome, Huntspill, Ilchester, Ilminster, Longport(?), Mark, Martock, Michael Borough(?), Minehead, North and South Petherton, Pawlett, Selwood(?), Shepton Mallet, Nether Stowey, Northover, "Somerset", Somerton, Stogursey, Tatton(?), Taunton, Weare, Wellington, Wells, Weston Zoyland, Wiveliscombe, Yeovil.
Victuallers' (Lenten) Recognizances (1572-1634).
Raleigh Wine Licences (1585-7, 1596-7).
Mompesson Licences (1620): Ashbrittle, Ashill, Axbridge, (South) Banwell, Bath, Bicknoller, Bishops Lydeard, Bradford, Breane, East Brent, Brewham, Bristol, Bruton, Camerton, Castle Cary, (Old) Chard, Charlton, Cheddar, Chinnock, Combe St. Nicholas, Creech St. Michael, Crewkerne, North Curry, Curry Rivel, Egarsley(?), Exford, Frome Sellwood, Glastonbury, Halton, Haslebury Plucknett, Hinton St. George, Ilminster, Keynsham, Kingsdon, Kingston Seymour, Martock, Merriott, Minehead, Neathersby(?), Norton Fitzwarren, Odcombe, Pensford, South Petherton, Pitminster, Shepton Beauchamp, Somerton, Staple Fitzpaine, Stogumber, Taunton, Thorne St. Margaret, Trull, Watchett, Wedmore, Wellington, Wells,

Somerset: *National Records* continued

Wincanton, Winsham, Wiveliscombe, Woolavington, Worle, Yeovil.
See below for original licences held locally.
Coventry Wine Licences (1626-39): Beckington, Bedminster, Bristol, Crockerne Pill, Farland in Wraxall, Glastonbury, Ilminster, Keynsham, Martock, Minehead, Pensford and Chew, North Petherton, Taunton, Wells.
Wine Licences: Pipe Office (1670-1756).

Somerset Archive and Record Service, *Taunton.*

1552-1828 Inns and Alehouses

Quarter Sessions records
Recognizance rolls from 1610 include tipplers.
Sessional rolls for 17th and early 18th centuries contain presentments etc.
Recognizance lists 1650-1829 (with gaps).

Bridgwater Borough records
Alehouse recognizances 1725-1737.

1828 on: Inns, Public Houses and Beer Shops

Quarter Sessions records
Notices of intention to apply for licence 1929-50.
Licensing maps, some held in application files.

Other County records
Lic Ctee mins 1905-1981; General orders and correspondence 1906-1930.

Petty Sessions records
Fee books, Ilminster alehouses 1826-1871.
Alehouse registers and application files: Bishops Lydeard 1935-46; Bridgwater Borough 1926-1964; Crewkerne 1872-1909; Dunster post-1902 -1956; Frome 1872-1982; Glastonbury Borough 1893-97; Ilminster 1872-92; Long Ashton 1861-1920; Shepton Mallet 1872-1965 (gaps); Taunton 1872-1897; Taunton 1901 (incl beer houses); Taunton Borough 1900-1901, 1906, 1929, 1946-55, 1956-1963 ; Wansdyke 1884-1982 (gaps); Wells City 1931-54; Weston-super-Mare 1903-91; Williton 1872-1963; Wiveliscombe 1900-1901; Yeovil Borough 1903-1921.
Lists of beer and cider licences: Ilminster 1830-69.
Alehouses licences: Dunster 1872-1956, 1959-64.

Other Licences
Mompesson licences for 18 inns, 1618-1620 [Q/RLa 34/1-4; DD/MR 116].
See also left under 'National records'.

Bath & North East Somerset Record Office.

1552-1828: Inns and Alehouses

Borough records
Borough Sessions books 1682-1776 contain annual lists of victuallers' recognizances.
Registers of alehouse recognizances 1772-1782, 1782-1789, 1806-14, 1824-32.
Alehouse recognizances, loose bundle, 1824-32.

Somerset: *Bath & North-East Somerset R.O.* ctd.

1828 on: Inns, Public Houses and Beer Shops

Bath Magistrates' Court: Licensing records
Special Sessions mins, incl licensing, 1851-68.
Licensing Sessions mins and reg of lics 1871-74.
Licensing Sessions mins , 5 vols, 1873-1904.
Licensing Session mins containing Transfer Sessions 1904-12, PS 1904-12, Special Sessions 1904-09, Occasional Lics 1904-09.
Licensing Sessions mins containing Lic Ctee 1907-1912, Compensation Authority 1907-11, Special Sessions 1907-12, PS 1908-13, Occasional Lics 1909-13.
Licensing Sessions mins containing Lic JPs 1912-1916, Compensation Authority 1912-16, Transfer Sessions 1912-16, PS 1914-16, Occasional Lics 1913-16.
Licensing Sessions mins, 2 vols 1917-34.
Transfer Sessions mins, 2 vols 1916-33.
Licensing Compensation Authority mins, 1916-34.
Petty Sessions: Mins of Lic ctee 1916-33.
Meetings of JPs, mins 1912-53.
Lic reg 1871-1902 (at front newspaper cuttings).
Licensing registers 1903-70.
Register of drunkenness, 2 pages, 1916.
List of applicants for renewal of licences, billiards, wines, beer and spirits, 1887-?1906.
Report on licensed houses in City of Bath 1903, 1912, 1923.
List of persons holding publicans' licences 1911.
List of publicans and spirit retailers 1928.

Weston (Bath) Petty Sessional Division records
Reg of lics: alehouses and beerhouses, billiards and wine (Keynsham as well as Weston Divisions) c.1940-54; Reg of Beerhouses, 1953-64; Reg of Alehouse licences 1953-65.

Other licences
Bath City, regs of music and dancng 1904-61; List of applicants for renewal of licences, billiards, wines, beer and spirits, 1887-?1906.

STAFFORDSHIRE

National Records (see pages 6-8)

Letters Patent (1554-71): Lichfield, Stafford, Wolverhampton.
Vintners' fines (1569-72): Stafford.
Victuallers' (Lenten) Recognizances (1572-1634).
Raleigh Wine Licences (1582-3, 1596-7).
Mompesson Licences (1620): Bilston, Norton, Uttoxeter, Wolverhampton.
Coventry Wine Licences (1634/5): Leek.
Wine Licences: Pipe Office (1670-1756).

Staffordshire continued

Staffordshire Record Office, *Stafford.*

1552-1828: Inns and Alehouses
Quarter Sessions
Sessions bundles from mid-16th century onwards contains occasional alehouses recognizances.
Reg of alehouse keepers for whole county 1782-1792.

1828 on: Inns, Public Houses and Beer Shops

Magistrates' Courts records
Cannock & Penkridge: Alehouse lics 1872-1900; Beerhouse lics 1872-1900; Alehouse/beerhouse lics 1901-37; Lics 1938-66; Licensing plans 1897-1948.
Cannock: Court records 1984-92.
Cheadle: Alehouse lics 1919-38.
Eccleshall: Court records 1903-17, 1939-54, 1959-78.
Leek: Court records 1903-06; Licensing plans 1875-1967.
Newcastle-under-Lyme Borough: Court records 1918-51, 1954-63.
Pirehill North Division (incl. Newcastle-under-Lyme and Stoke, Burslem and Fenton, parts of Stoke on Trent): Court records 1872-1978.
Rugeley: Court records 1872-89, 1903-72, 1984-92.
Seisdon: Court records 1984-92.
Stafford Borough: Lics 1872-1904; 1937-75.
Stafford County: Lics 1872-1938; Eccleshall Div lics 1894-1903, 1919-75.
Stone: Court records 1907-17, 1939-79.
Stoke on Trent: Burslem Borough lics 1927-76; Hanley Borough lics 1872-1976; Longton Borough lics 1885-72; Stoke on Trent Borough lics 1902-1976; Stoke on Trent County 1950, 1969-73.
(Stoke) Tunstall: Court records 1915-46.
Tamworth Borough: Court records 1911-54.
Tamworth Petty Sessions: Court records 1954-68.
Uttoxeter: Court records 1889-1979.
Winecote Petty Sessions (then Co. Warw.) 1918-65.

Birmingham Central Library, City Archives

Register of alehouse and beer house licences, Parish of Handsworth 1807-11.

Lichfield Record Office

Petty Sessions registers
Burton upon Trent Div: JPs' mins, Special Sessions for transferring of lics and Brewster Sessions 1871-96, 1949-56; Lic regs 1888-1958.
City & County of Lichfield: lics 1923-74; music, dancing, billiards 1954-62.
Lichfield & Brownhills: lics 1959-74.

Magistrates' Court records
Burton on Trent Borough: Compensation Authority mins 1905-1961; Lic regs 1888-1962.

Dudley Archives and Local History Service,
Coseley, Dudley.

Petty Sessions records
Kingswinford and Wordsley PS Div (amal with Dudley in 1966): Regs of lics, 7 vols, 1872-58.

Sandwell Community History and Archives Service, Smethwick Library

Magistrate's Court Records: Inns and Alehouses
Smethwick 1904-66.
Rowley Regis 1903-64.
Oldbury 1884-1963.
West Bromwich 1874-1986.
Qednesbury 1961-66.
Tipton 1919-38, 1959-66.

Wolverhampton Archives & Local Studies,
Wolverhampton.

Magistrates' Courts records
Wolverhampton Borough: Lics 1872-1917.
Wolverhampton County: Bilston and Sedgley Div lics 1873-1931; Tettenhall Div lics 1939-58.
Licensing plans, 19th/20th century.

SUFFOLK

Boroughs which were their own licensing authority:
Bury St Edmunds.
Licensing Divisions, post-1828:
Blything, Eye, Framlingham, Felixstowe, Hartismere, Hoxne, Ipswich, Orwell, Stow, and Woodbridge

National Records (see pages 6-8)

Letters Patent (1554-71): Brockford(?), Ipswich, Lavenham, Long Melford, Newmarket, Sudbury.
Vintners' fines (1569-72): Bungay, Framlingham, Hadleigh, Halesworth, Lowestoft, Snape Bridge, Sudbury, Wickham (Hadleigh), Woodbridge.
Victuallers' (Lenten) Recognizances (1572-1634).
Raleigh Wine Licences (1582-3, 1584-6, 1596-7, 1600-1).
Mompesson Licences (1620): Alderton, Bardwell, Barking cum Needham, Barnby, Bawdsey, Baylham, Beccles, Bedfield, East Bergholt, Bildeston, Botesdale, Boxford, Bradfield, Bramfield, Bramford, Great Bradley, Little Bretton(?), Great Brissett, Bungay, Burwell Ashe(?), Bury St. Edmunds, Butley, Buxhall, Cavendish, Chelmondiston, Clare, Coddenham, Combs, Copdock, Copthorne(?), Cotton, Debenham, Denston, Dinnington, Dunstall(?), Dunwich, Easton or Euston, Elden, Elmswell, Eye, Eyke, Felixstowe, Felsham, Great Finborough, Finningham, Fornham, Fornham All Saints, Framlingham, Glemsford, Great and Little Glenham, Glomesbury(?), Hacheston, Hadleigh, Halesworth, Hartest, Haughley, Herringfleet, Hintlesham, Hitcham, Higham, Holborne(?), Hollesley, Hopton, Hoxne, Hundon, Ipswich, Ixworth, Kentford, Kersey, Kirton, Langham, Layham, Leiston, Lewerware(?), Lidgate, Mendham, Mendlesham, Metfield, Middleton, Nayland, Needham Market (Barking), Palgrave, Parham, Peasenhall, Rickinghall, Rougham, Rushmere, St. Mary Tower(?), Shotley, Soame(?), Somersham, Stanton, Stoke, Stoke juxta Nayland, Little Stoneham,

Suffolk: *National Records*, *Mompesson lics* contd.

Stowmarket, Stradbroke, Stratford, Sudbury, Sutton, Sweffling, Thorpe, Great Thurlow, Trimley, Tuddenham, Ufford, Walberswick, Walpole, Walton, Wangford, Weeke(?), Weybread, Wickhambrook, Wickham Market, Woodbridge, Worlingworth, Wrentham, Yaxley.
Coventry Wine Licences (1626-39): Aldeburgh, Brandon Ferry, Brantham and East Bergholt, Bury St Edmunds, Homersfield, Ipswich, Lowestoft, Needham Market and Creeting and Baylham, St Olives[?], Sudbury, Walberswick, Woodbridge, Yoxford.
Wine Licences: Pipe Office (1670-1756).

| Suffolk Record Office, Ipswich Branch. |

1552-1828: Inns and Alehouses
Quarter Sessions records
Sessions Order Book 1639-1651 contains presentments etc.
Original recognizances 1800.
Petition from Mutford and Lothingland against refusal to license additional beerhouse.

1828 on: Inns, Public Houses and Beer Shops
Quarter Sessions records
Certificates of real occupation, beer licence,10 applications, Haverhill 1847-48.
Licensing maps and plans, Cookley, Pakefield, Saxmundham, Parham, Lowestoft 1910-1912.

Other County records
Licensing court minutes, Ipswich 1954-1962.
East Suffolk Lic Ctee papers 1874-1902.
Agenda 1906; memo and amendments post-1911.

Petty Sessions records
Registers of licences Blything Div 1874-1940; Eye 1897-1967; Felixstowe 1936-63; Framlingham 1934-56; Hartismere 1918-62; Hoxne Div 1913-1968; Ipswich 1910-77; Orwell 1956-73; Stow 1940-75; Woodbridge 1904-63.

Other licensing activities
Petty Sessions records
Music and dancing lic reg: Felixstowe 1935-74; Ipswich 1910-59; Woodbridge 1904-74.

| Suffolk Record Office, Bury St Edmunds Branch. |

1552-1828: Inns and Alehouses

Bury St. Edmunds Borough records:
Publicans' recognizances 1799-1818; Lists of publicans c.1783-1802; Printed notices by mayor enforcing Sunday closing 1846, 1854.

Petty Sessions records
Registers of licences: Blackbourn Div 1921-66; Bury St. Edmunds Borough 1904-75; Lackford 1872-1964; Melford 1936-57; Newmarket 1970-75; Risbridge 1900-74; Sudbury Borough 1872-1957; Sudbury and Cosford Division 1970-74; Thingoe and Thedwastre 1892-1966.

Other licensing activities
Petty Sessions
Music and dancing lic reg: Sudbury and Cosford 1960-74.

| Suffolk Record Office, Lowestoft Branch. |

The Office holds records for two distinct areas - Lowestoft Borough Petty Sessions Division and the Mutford and Lothingland Petty Sessions Division.

1552-1828: Inns and Alehouses

Adair Family and Estate Collection
Copy form for alehouse licence including articles to be observed, 16th century [741/HA12/B1/4/18].
Grant for alehouse recognizance to William Mosse with list of articles to be observed, 1610 [741/HA12B1/1/7].
Licence to Thomas Pampnett to keep an alehouse in Bungay, 1616 [741/HA12B1/4/63].

1828 on: Inns, Public Houses and Beer Shops

Borough records
Southwold: Regs of lics to sell alcohol 1872-1929.
Lowestoft: Lic ctee mins 1924-37; Lic sub-ctee mins 1942-47.

Petty Sessions records
Lowestoft Borough PS Division: Mins and Court regs have occasional refs; Police reports on criminal cases, general orders and corres on licensing mattters, posters re notices of Special Sessions, press cuttings re the 1904 Compensation Act.
Mutford and Lothingland PS Division: Mins and Court regs have occasional refs to lics and extensions, also transferring beerhouse lics ; Regs of lics, 1871 onwards; Lists of applicants for certs under the 1869 Wine and Beerhouse Act etc, and a list of lic'd premises; Police reports on criminal cases, general orders and corres on lic matters, posters re notices of Special Sessions.

Other licences
Petty Sessions
Lowestoft Borough PS, posters re music, singing and dancing lics.
Mutford and Lothingland PS, as above.

SURREY

Boroughs which were their own licensing authority: Guildford, Kingston.
Licensing Districts post-1828:
Chertsey, Croydon, Dorking, Epsom, Farnham, Godstone, Guildford, Kingston, Newington, Reigate, Richmond, Wimbledon.

| National Records (see pages 6-8) |

Letters Patent (1554-71): Bermondsey, Croydon, Guildford, Kingston, Newington, Redryft(?), Southwark.
Vintners' fines (1569-72): None.
Victuallers' (Lenten) Recognizances (1572-1634).
Raleigh Wine Licences (1582-3, 1584-5, 1586-7).

Surrey: *National Records* continued

Mompesson Licences (1620): Alfold, Bagshot, Bletchingley, Great Bookham, Carshalton, Chertsey, Croydon, Dunsfold, Egham, Ewhurst, Farnham, Godalming, Godstone, Haslemere, West Horsley, Kingston, Leatherhead, Leigh, Limpsfield, Lingfield, Putney, Reigate, Richmond, St. Mary Newington, Southwark, Streatham, Sutton, Walton, Weybridge.
See 'Surrey Innkeepers licensed by Sir Giles Mompesson 1618-20', J. Hunter, *Root & Branch* (West Surrey FHS) **14**, p.142.

Coventry Wine Licences (1626-39): Battersea, Blackmanstreet [?], Bletchingley, Byfleet, Chertsey, Croydon, Dorking, Ewell, Godalming, Godstone, Guildford, Kingston, Lambeth, Mitcham, Mortlake, Moulsey, Peckham, Reigate, Richmond, Wandsworth, Weybridge.

Wine Licences: Pipe Office (1670-1756).

Surrey History Centre, Woking.

1552-1828: Inns and Alehouses

Quarter Sessions records
Sessions Order Books 1659-1828 contain a few recognizances, petitions, presentments etc con-cerned with licensing and orders for suppression.
Sessional rolls and bundles 1660-99 include a few presentments, informations and petitions.
Victuallers' registers 1785-1827.

Petty Sessions records
Hundreds of Copthorne and Effingham mins 1784-1793. Published in West Surrey FHS Record Series **8**, ed. C.R. Webb, 1989.
Hundreds of Kingston and Elmbridge mins 1752-94;

Guildford Borough Records
Draft Court Book 1698-1734 contains some recognizances; Regs of victuallers' recogs 1735-1809, 1815-28; Bundles of victuallers' recogs 1780-82, 1792-97, 1799, 1800, 1802-04, 1807; Victuallers' lics 1777-1824.

Family papers
Loseley MSS includes applications for alehouse licences, lists of applications and petitions 1570s, mainly south west Surrey [LM 1027-1034].

Carew family papers
Late 16th-early 17th century contain stray papers from clerk of peace, Brixton and Wallington Hundred [643, 663].

1828 on: Inns, Public Houses and Beer Shops

Quarter Sessions records
Sessions orders and bundles 1828 onwards contain occasional applications for new licences and general orders.
County Lic ctee records: Mins, mainly dealing with Newington Div 1873-1935; Chairman's Books contain notes on individual lic'd premises, reports and opinions 1873-1904; Agenda Book 1909-15

contains names of premises to be considered for lic renewal, annual list of lics refused, compensation money details.
Return of Surrey Licensed Houses 1892, 1904, ptd.

Petty Sessions records
Guildford Bench volume 1840-61 incl lic meetings.

Other licensing activities
Quarter Sessions records
Applications for music and dancing lics for London part of Surrey, 1880s.

Kingston Museum & Heritage Service.

1552-1828: Inns and Alehouses
Hundreds of Kingston and Elmbridge Petty Sessions minute book 1723-51 [KS2/1/1].
Bailiffs' Minute Books have references to licensing, of alehouses 1705-79 [KE2/5/1 5].
Petition from C H Rowlls to licensing justices early 19th century [KE2/6/2].

1828 on: Inns, Public Houses and Beer Shops
JPs' mins 1882-1939; Mins 1939-79; JPs' meeting mins 1896-1972; Victuallers lic book 1828-96; Licensing JPs' mins 1897-1972; Lic mins 1941-68; Regs of lics 1897-1963; licensing JPs' plans 1897-1948.

London Metropolitan Archives
(formerly Corporation of London Records Office).

1552-1828: Inns and Alehouses

Borough of Southwark:
Precepts of licensing victuallers in Southwark 1755-65; Victuallers' lics 1743-67; Southwark QS Order Book 1789; Sessions Book for licensing sessions 1785-1791; Rolls of victuallers' recogs.
'Candid Enquiry into the Right of Jurisdiction of the City of London over the Borough of Southwark' (1787) highlighted the dispute between the City and Surrey justices over licensing. From 1792 licensing of Southwark victuallers was left to Surrey justices.

Bodleian Library, Oxford.

Journal of Bostock Fuller of Tandridge Court 1608-1622 refers to licensing alehouses out of Sessions.

Wandsworth Library.

Minutes of the justices of peace for the western half of the Brixton Hundred 1786-1822, 1822-69.

See also 'Licensed Houses in Wandsworth, 1786', Jim Devine, *East Surrey FHS* **17.2** (March 1994). List of licensees and premises.

Note. No relevant records are held by the *Minet Library* (L.B. of Lambeth), *Merton Library Service* or *Southwark Local Studies Library*.

See also under 'Middlesex: *London Metropolitan Archives*' (formerly *GLRO*), page 34, for places in Surrey which were part of the metropolis.

SUSSEX

Boroughs which were their own licensing authority: Chichester, Hastings, Rye, Pevensey, Seaford, Winchelsea.

Licensing Districts post-1828:
Arundel Borough, Arundel, Brighton, Chichester City, Chichester, Eastbourne, Frant, East Grinstead, Hailsham, Haywards Heath, Horsham, Lewes, Midhurst, Petworth, Rye, Rye Borough, Steyning, Uckfield.

National Records (see pages 6-8)

Letters Patent (1554-71): Chichester, Harting, Lewes, Rye.
Vintners' fines (1569-72): Chichester, East Grinstead, Horsham, Lewes.
Victuallers' (Lenten) Recognizances (1572-1634).
Raleigh Wine Licences (1596-7?).
Mompesson Licences (1620): Battle, Chichester, Chiltington, Cuckfield, Dallington, Felpham, Findon, Houghton, Lewes, Lodsworth, Mayfield, Midhurst, Petworth, Pulborough, Rudgwick, Slindon, Steyning, Uckfield, Wadhurst, Winchelsea.
Coventry Wine Licences (1626-39): Arundel, Chiltington, Forest Row, Hastings, Lewes, Maresfield, Midhurst, Petworth, Steyning.
Wine Licences: Pipe Office (1670-1756).

East Sussex Record Office, *Lewes.*

1552-1828: Inns and Alehouses

Quarter Sessions records
Sessions rolls contain petitions and recognizances. A separate series of recognizances for the period 1775 to 1827 were destroyed before 1832.
Enrolled recognizances:
Hasting Rape 1627-1713 and 1781;
North Pevensey Rape 1632-1716 and 1781;
South Pevensey Rape 1664-1713 and 1781.

Borough records
Pevensey: Annual list of victuallers' recogs 1731-39, 1761, 1763-69; Recogs 1800-28.
Rye: Enrolled recogs to 1772; Recog book 1772-1815; Lenten recogs 1586; Lists of fines for lics 1680-1737; Case for the opinion of Counsel concerning licensing and old house 1779.
Seaford: An alehouse recognizance for tippler 1584; Certs of good character 1795.
Winchelsea: Recogs and lics 1775-1822; Notice of change of licensee, Jolly Sailor Inn, Icklesham, 1812; Notice of next licensing meeting endorsed with names of licensees n.d.; Informations re sale of liquor without a licence 1775-76, 1796.

1828 on: Inns, Public Houses and Beer Shops

Eastern Sussex Quarter Sessions
Mins of Lic Ctee 1873-1952; Reg of applications for confirmation of lics 1872-1904; Applications for lics 1872-1961; Licensing Ctee letter books 1872-1936; East Sussex Lic Compensation Authority letter books 1905-36.

Petty Sessions records
Battle: Lic regs 1921-56.
Bexhill: Alehouse lic regs. 1928-56; Beerhouse lic reg. 1928-56.
Brighton: Lic regs 1822-1968; Mins of the annual lic meetings 1925-49; Mins of the ctee on licensed houses 1902-05 and notes of surrendered lics 1902-61; Plans of licensed premises 1919-54; mins of licensing ctee for alterations to licensed premises 1948-89.
Burwash: Lic regs 1931-74.
Eastbourne: Lic regs 1886-1967; Mins of the Lic Compensation Authority 1926-71.
Frant (Mark Cross): Lic regs 1872-1973.
Hailsham: Lic regs 1886-1970.
Hastings Borough: Lic regs 1872-76; Alehouse lic regs 1877-1956; Beerhouse lic regs 1877-1956 ; Mins of the Licensing Compensation Authority 1902-51.
Hastings (County): Lic regs 1872-98; Alehouse lic regs 1898-1928 ; Beerhouse lic regs 1898-1928.
Hastings: Alehouse & beerhouse lic regs 1974-77.
Hove Borough: Lic regs 1905-35.
Hove County: Lic regs 1858-1922, 1967-74.
Hove: Lic regs 1974-86.
Lewes: Lic regs 1872-1966; mins of Lic ctee 1952-1967; plans of lic premises 1943-c1987.
Rye Borough: Lic regs 1903-58.
Uckfield: Lic regs 1872-1974.

Borough records
Hastings Quarter Sessions records (C20 to 1971) Reg of lodging house keepers 1900-24.
Rye: Notices to overseers and constables of proposed applications for lics 1831-32; Petitions to JPs for licences with certs of good character 1831-1832; Petitions against granting new lics 1831; Notices to overseers and constables, petitions with certs re transfers and renewals 1835-40.
Seaford: Petition for lic for Terminus Hotel 1863 .

Other licences
Music and dancing licence registers: Battle 1973-74, 1979-82; Eastbourne 1921-67; Hastings Borough 1950-74; Hastings 1974-82; Hove Borough 1967-1974; Hove County 1967-74; Hove 1974-82; Lewes 1924-76; Rye 1979-81.
Club registers: Battle 1915-74; Bexhill 1929-61; Brighton 1902-58; Eastbourne 1903-14; Frant (Mark Cross) 1906-61; Hailsham 1903-62; Hastings Borough 1903-74; Hastings County 1903-1928; Hastings 1974-77; Hove Borough 1962-74; Hove County 1962-74; Hove 1974-86; Lewes 1963-87; Rye County 1903-61; Uckfield 1936-62.

West Sussex Record Office, *Chichester.*

1552-1828: Inns and Alehouses

Quarter Sessions records
Sessions Rolls 1594-1828; Order Books 1642-1828. Contain presentments, petitions, indictments, also certificates of good behaviour, general orders etc.

Sussex: *West Sussex Record Office*, continued

Borough records
Chichester: Sessions Rolls 1577-1827. Contain presentments of unlicensed alehouses.

1828 on: Inns, Public Houses and Beer Shops

Quarter Sessions records
Regs of applications for confirmation of lics 1872-1904; Lic Ctee mins 1873-1971; Applications for lics 1898-1961; Letter Books 1905-15 ; Licensing map, Borough of Chichester *c.*1958.

Petty Sessions records
Licensing registers: Arundel Borough 1863-1916; Arundel PS Div 1893-1969; Chichester City 1872-1953; Chichester PS Div. 1871-1953; East Grinstead PS Div 1945-69; Haywards Heath PS Div 1872-1965; Horsham PS Div 1897-1918, 1956-1970; Midhurst PS Div 1872-1956; Petworth PS Div 1872-1912, 1939-58; Steyning PS Div 1933-62.
Minute Books (Licensing): Arundel PS Div 1824-1966.
Court papers, incl lic papers: Midhurst PS Div 1943-1972; Petworth PS Div 1923-72.
Plans of lic'd premises: Petworth PS Div 1928-64.
Licensing returns: Midhurst PS Div 1947-72.

Police records
Chichester City Police and PS Div Lic reg 1901-50.

Other licences

Petty Sessions records
Music and dancing regs: Haywards Heath PS Div 1939-65; Steyning PS Div 1934-42, incl other lics.

WARWICKSHIRE

Boroughs which were their own licensing authority: Warwick.

National Records (see pages 6-8)

Letters Patent (1554-71): Coventry.
Vintners' fines (1569-72): Birmingham, Stratford, Tamworth.
Victuallers' (Lenten) Recognizances (1572-1634).
Raleigh Wine Licences (1582-5, 1586-7, 1595-7).
Mompesson Licences (1620): Stratford upon Avon.
Coventry Wine Licences (1626-39): Alcester, Birmingham, Bromwich, Coleshill, Warwick.
Wine Licences: Pipe Office (1670-1756).

Warwickshire County Record Office, *Warwick.*

1552-1828: Inns and Alehouses

Quarter Sessions records
Original recognizances, annual bundles by hundred, some years missing or incomplete 1661-1740, 1753-1828.
Victuallers' registers, some missing, 1753-1828.
Order books, mins and indictments books, 17th century, contain some references to victuallers.

Warwickshire: *County Record Office* continued

Quarter Session continued
Index to licensed victuallers and public houses in Warwickshire, 1801-28, compiled by volunteers from QS registers of victuallers' recognizances. On-line
<www.warwickshire.gov/uk/countyrecordoffice>

Borough records
Warwick victuallers' recogs 1572-73, 1595-6.

1828 on: Inns, Public Houses and Beer Shops

Quarter Sessions records
Returns to Home Office 1906-54; Licensing plans and applications, 23 bundles 1900-1925; Lic ctee mins etc, from 1872, mainly 20th century.

Petty Sessions records
Lic regs: Solihull 1837-1903; for many PS Divs, between 1872 and 1981.

The Shakespeare Centre Library and Archives, *Stratford on Avon.*

Lists of victuallers: Stratford on Avon 1604-6, 1745, 1758, 1753-85, 1787-1809, 1811-14, 1821-28; Barlichway Hundred 1814-15, 1821, 1824, 1827, 1834, 1836, 1839-44; Barlichway Hundred, Stratford on Avon and Snitterfield Div 1846-61, 1864-67, 1869-1871, 1873-83.

Coventry Local History Centre.

1552-1828: Inns and Alehouses
Coventry Quarter Sessions records
Mins for licensing victuallers 1745-52, 1776-82, 1808-35;
List of lic'd alehouse keepers and victuallers 1609.

1828 on: Inns, Public Houses and Beer Shops
Magistrates' Court records of City of Coventry
Lic ctee mins 1949-68; Licensing plans 1926-77; Regs of intoxicating liquor licences 1878-1956.

Other licences
Regs of lics for music, singing and dancing 1891-1900, 1942-64.

Birmingham Central Library, City Archives.

Lic ctee mins (various) 1872-1920 (gaps).
Plans of the licensing justices for public houses and hotel, Birmingham, 19th/20th century.
No licensing registers appear to survive.

See also under Staffordshire: Handsworth.

WESTMORLAND

Boroughs which were their own licensing authority: Kendal.
Licensing Districts post-1828:
  Ambleside, East Ward, Kendal Borough, Kendal Ward, Kirkby Lonsdale, West Ward, Windermere.

National Records (see pages 6-8)

Letters Patent (1554-71): None.
Vintners' fines (1569-72): None.
Victuallers' (Lenten) Recognizances (1572-1634).
Raleigh Wine Licences (1582-3, 1583-4, 1595-6).
Mompesson Licences (1620): None.
Coventry Wine Licences (1636): Kirkby Lonsdale.
Wine Licences: Pipe Office (1670-1756).

Cumbria County Record Office, *Kendal.*

1552-1828: Inns and Alehouses

Quarter Sessions records
Original recogs 1809-24; Alehouse register 1822.

Kendal Borough records
Kendal Quarter Sessions order books 1685-1731 are concerned with licensing, but not calendared.

Fleming of Rydal Family papers
Contain misc papers concerning alehouses 1634-95 [WD/Ry/Boxes 33-35].

1828 on: Inns, Public Houses and Beer Shops

Quarter Sessions records
Licensing committee papers 1872-77.
Registers of licences, QS: Kendal and Lonsdale Wards 1873-74; East and West Wards 1873-77.
Registers of licences (Intoxicating liquor laws):
  Ambleside 1878-1967; East Ward 1881-1967; Kendal Borough 1947-66; Kendal Ward 1880-1967; Kirkby Lonsdale 1893-1967; West Ward 1855-1967; Windermere 1894-1967.

Petty Sessions records
Registers of licences: Ambleside and Windermere 1922-48; East Ward (Kirby Stephen) 1909-14; Hawkshead 1903-75; Kendal Borough 1919-54 ; Kendal Ward 1903-57; Lonsdale Ward 1903-55.

Borough records
Kendal Borough Police report *c.*1895.

Other licences
Petty Sessions records
Ambleside and Windermere Division, files re music and dancing licensing 1970-72.

WILTSHIRE

Boroughs which were their own licensing authority: Marlborough.
Licensing Districts post-1828:
  Bradford on Avon, Calne, Chippenham, Cricklade, Devizes borough, Devizes county, Everley and Pewsey, Malmesbury, Marlborough borough, Marlborough county, Melksham, Salisbury City, Salisbury and Amesbury, Swindon borough, Swindon county, Tisbury and Mere, Trowbridge, Warminster, Whorwellsdown.

National Records (see pages 6-8)

Letters Patent (1554-71): Malmesbury, Salisbury, Warbleston(?).
Vintners' fines (1569-72): Bradford, Calne, Clack (in Lyneham), Chippenham, Devizes, Easton, Highworth, Hindon, Malmesbury, Marlborough, Salisbury, Trowbridge, Warminster, Wilton.
Victuallers' (Lenten) Recognizances (1572-1634).
Raleigh Wine Licences (1583-6, 1593-4, 1595-7).
Mompesson Licences (1620): Aldbourne, Amesbury, Bishops Canning, Bradford on Avon, Bratton, Burbage, Castle Combe, Chapmans-lade(?), Charnam Street(?), Chilton Foliatt, Corsham, Devizes, Fisherton, Hinden, Keevil, Lea, Lees Marsh(?), Lyneham, Ludgershall, Market Lavington, Maddington, Marlborough, Salisbury ('New Sarum'), Seales(?), Shrewton, Sowerton, Steeple Langford, Swindon, Trowbridge, Warminster, Westbury, Williborn(?).
Coventry Wine Licences (1626-39): Amesbury, Bromham, Calne, Castle Combe, Chippenham, Highworth, Lavington, 'Ludwell', Malmesbury, Potterne, Salisbury, Warminster, Wilton.
Wine Licences: Pipe Office (1670-1756).

Wiltshire & Swindon Archives, *Chippenham.*

1552-1828: Inns and Alehouses

Quarter Sessions records
Original recogs 1739-69; Earlier original recogs enrolled on Great Rolls; Original recognizances, Amesbury Division, 1808, 1814, and Highworth, Cricklade, Staple and Kingsbridge Division, 1828.
Register of recognizances 1756-61, 1822-27.

Borough records
Devizes: Lic ctee mins 1790-1819.
Marlborough: Two memoranda of the licensing of victualllers 1724, 1731.
Note of victuallers licensed in sessions 1732-33.

1828 on: Inns, Public Houses and Beer Shops

Quarter Sessions records
Lic Ctee mins, acs, corres 1872-1981.

Petty Sessions records
Registers of licences: Devizes Borough 1867-1968; Marlborough Borough 1903-53; Salisbury City 1932-1975; Swindon Borough 1919-64; Bradford-on-Avon (county) 1952-69; Calne (county) 1872-1974;

Wiltshire: *Wiltshire & Swindon Archives,*
1828-on, continued

Petty Sessions ctd: Chippenham (county) 1872-
1974; Cricklade (county) 1947-74; Devizes
(county) 1865-1968; Everley and Pewsey (county)
1903-61; Malmesbury (county) 1911-74;
Marlborough (county) 1872-1974; Melksham
(county) 1891-1968; Salisbury and Amesbury
(county) 1947-75; Swindon (county) 1922-83;
Tisbury and Mere (county) 1872-1951; Trowbridge
(county) 1936-66; Warminster (county) 1872-1949;
Whorwellsdown (county) 1936-44.
Lic Ctee mins: Devizes Borough 1842-66; Swindon
Borough 1910-60; Chippenham (county) 1949-69.

Other licences
Music and dancing lic regs: Devizes Borough 1934-
1956; Salisbury City 1942-61; Swindon Borough
1893-1965; Chippenham (county) 1966-82;
Everley and Pewsey (county) 1961-82;
Malmesbury (county) 1966-82; Marlborough
(county) 1966-82; Swindon (county) 1922-83.

WORCESTERSHIRE

National Records (see pages 6-8)

Letters Patent (1554-71): Hevysham(?), Worcester.
Vintners' fines (1569-72): Broadway, Bromsgrove,
Driotwich, Kidderminster, Shipston on Stour,
Worcester.
Victuallers' (Lenten) Recognizances (1572-1634).
*Raleigh Wine Licences (1582-4, 1585-6, 1587-8,
1589-90, 1594-7).*
Mompesson Licences (1620): Bewdley, Bredon,
Bromsgrove, Evesham, Inkberrow, Kings Norton,
Great Malvern, Martin Hussingtree, Shipston upon
Stour, Sidbury(?), Worcester.
Coventry Wine Licences (1626-39): Droitwich,
Evesham, Ombersley, Shipston on Stour,
Worcester.
Wine Licences: Pipe Office (1670-1756).

Worcestershire Record Office, Worcester.

1552-1828: Inns and Alehouses

Official papers of the Lord Keeper Thomas Coventry
Lics to sell wine 1626-39 (604) (indexed transcript,
see Introduction, page 7); tobacco 1633-34.

Quarter Sessions records
Quarter Sessions rolls 1591-1890. These are
calendared and indexed 1591-1643, and available
on open shelves [HQq 942.44002].
Sessions Order Books 1693-1951. Indexed 1693-
1802, available on open shelves; Vols 1-5, 1693-
1790 have references to alehouses and ale selling;
Vol 3, 1732-56 to liquors, spirituous.
Recognizance Book 1700-04.

Worcestershire: *Worcs. Record Office,* contd

Worcester City:
Warrants and papers concerning licensing of
alehouses 1770-1834
[class 850 Hanley Castle BA 8119 parcel 6 (i)].
Receipts, accounts, warrants and other papers
concerning licensing etc 1724-1831
[850 Hanley Castle BA 8119 parcel 8 (viii)].

Bewdley Borough records
Alehouse recogs 1727, 1818, 1821 and 1824-28.

1828 on: Inns, Public Houses and Beer Shops

Quarter Sessions records
Sessions Orders 1852-1880, and index.
County Lic Ctee, letters, agendas and papers,
accounts, corres and one plan 1872-1919.
Papers re Law case, Crown v JPs of Worcs re
licensing hours in Upton-upon-Severn 1904.
Papers re licensing appeal. Transfer of lics 1883.
Papers re Elton appeal, Licensing Act 1872, 1884.
Maps showing 'populous places' and locations of
PHs 1893-1912.
Lic Ctee mins 1905.
Plans of two PHs in Oldbury 1921.
Plans and other papers re application for lic,
Cakemore, 1906.
Lic Ctee corres c.1910-on; Lic Ctee mins 1905-51.
County Confirming and Compensation Ctee mins
1952-61; Corres re closing down Worcs. PHs
1956-1963; Licensing Ctee Compensation Fund,
Treasurer's account 1905-26; County
Compensation Ctee mins 1961.

Other County records
County Council Lic Ctee mins 1969-1974.
County Compensation Ctee:
Mins 1972-73; Unweeded and unclassified corres
1964-71.

Petty Sessions records
Droitwich PS Div: Regs of lics, Droitwich Borough
1931-53; Regs of lics, Droitwich County 1915-71.
Evesham and Pershore PS Div: Regs of lics:
Pershore 1928-74; Evesham 1903-1954; Evesham
Borough 1903-51 ; Evesham 1954-74.
Halesowen PS Div: Regs of lics mainly for sale of
beer and spirits, 1872-1934, with index.
Redditch PS Div: Regs of lics 1926-74.
Stourbridge PS Div: Reg of lics 1903-27; Reg of lics
1928-43.
Upton upon Severn PS Div: Reg of lics for PHs
1879-1901; Books of recogs 1894-1938.
Worcester PS Div: Reg of lic'd premises 1876-1928.

Other licences
Registers of music and dancing: Pershore 1965-9;
Evesham 1965-9; Redditch 1943-65, 1965-74;
Halesowen 1926-41

Worcester City:
Three notices to constables relating to meetings to ...
and license inns etc 1833-4
[x989.485 Cofton Hackett [microfilm] BA 7642 (ii)].

Worcestershire: *County Record Office* continued

Worcester City, **1828-on** continued
Notice to constable concerning granting licences to innkeepers 1834
[894.85 Cofton Hackett BA 8477 parcel 8].
Eleven tobacco, beer, cider, perry and brewers licences issued to Henry Bird of Bretfortin 1831-52 [705.353 BA 8163 parcel 3 (iii)].
Lists of lics for alehouses in Kidderminster Division and depositions in respect of cases to be heard in this division 1876 [705:55 BA 5278 parcel 19 (iv)].
Summonses re provisions of Beer Order 1920 [705:223 BA 8835 parcel 4 (iv) 24-26].
JPs' licences and forms of renewal and transfer of justices licences to hold an excise licence and for public dancing, singing and music re Crown Hotel [705:223 BA 8835 parcel 4 (iv) 27-91].

Dudley Archives and Local History Service,
Coseley, Dudley.

Dudley Magistrates Court records
Licensing Committee mins, 3 vols, 1909-64; Mins of Compensation Authority 1909-36; Mins of JPs acting as Confirming Authority under 1910 Act 1946-50.
Regs of lics 1904-41; List of lic'd premises 1908-13.
Treasurers' account: Compensation Fund 1905-34.
Plans of licensed premises 1900-07.

Other licences
Dudley, registers of music and dancing 1894-1941, 1920-64.

YORKSHIRE

National Records (see pages 6-8)

Letters Patent (1554-71): Beverley, Kingston upon Hull, Knaresborough, Richmond, Ripon, Westbridge(?), Wetherby, York.
Vintners' fines (1569-72): Bedale, Beverley, Boroughbridge, Cawood, Doncaster, Howden, Kingston upon Hull, New Malton, Northallerton, Pocklington, Richmond, Ripon, Selby, Sheffield, Snaith, Tadcaster, Topcliffe, Wetherby, Whitby, York.
Victuallers' (Lenten) Recognizances (1572-1634).
Raleigh Wine Licences (1582-7, 1588-9, 1595-7).
Mompesson Licences (1620): Folby(?), Leaninge Lane(?), Richmond, Wetherby.
Coventry Wine Licences (1626-39): South Cave, Doncaster, 'Fowlforth', Keighley, Kingston upon Hull, Kirkburn, Knaresborough, Leeds, Luddenden, New Malton, Otley, Pickeringleigh, Pocklington, Ripley, Ripon, Scarborough, Selby, Settrington, Sheffield, Stamford Bridge, Sutton, Wakefield, Wetherby, Whitby, Yarm, York.
Wine Licences: Pipe Office (1670-1756).

YORKSHIRE: YORK

National records: see under 'Yorkshire', left.

York City Archives Department, *York.*

1552-1828: Inns and Alehouses

York City records
Mins, 1559-1706, contain refs to lics and licensees.
House Books 1476-1706 contain occasional general statements.
Lists of recogs 1552-60, 1586-1605, 1646-48, 1650, 1660, 1663-63, 1720-37, 1754-56, 1763-1803.
Original recogs (few); Certs of good character (few).
Chamberlains' account books 1520-1830 record fines for licensing offences.

York Innholders' Company records
Admissions to the Company, petitions etc 1593-1824.

1828 on: Inns, Public Houses and Beer Shops

York City records
Regs of full lics 1908-32; Regs of beer house lics 1908-32; Watch ctee books 1870-1952 contain records of applications for lics; Lic ctee mins 1905-1950.

Police records
Reports 1843, 1902.

Licences for other activities
York City records
House books contain lists of wine retailers licensed by the Council during the reigns of Mary I and Elizabeth I.

Borthwick Institute, *York.*

1552-1828: Inns and Alehouses
York Innholders' Company accounts 1633-1778.

1828 on: Inns, Public Houses and Beer Shops
Parish records: Transfers of licences to sell intoxicating liquor addressed to Overseers of Parish of York 1846-64 [PR Y/HTK 38].

YORKSHIRE: EAST RIDING

Boroughs which were their own licensing authority: Beverley, Hedon, Kingston-upon-Hull.
Licensing Districts post-1828:
Bainton Beacon, Buckrose, Dickering, North, Middle and South Holderness, Holme Beacon, Howdenshire, North and South Hunsley, Ouse and Derwent, Wilton Beacon.

National records: see under 'Yorkshire', left.

Yorkshire: East Riding continued

East Riding of Yorkshire Archive Office, *Beverley.*

1552-1828: Inns and Alehouses

East Riding Quarter Sessions records
Sessions Order Books, occasional refs 1647-1651, 1708-1828; Reg of recogs on granting lics to keep inns or victualling houses 1822-28; Alehouse recogs, lists of lics, and certs of ministers and inhabitants supporting applications. Arranged according to Divs (incomplete) 1754-1826.

Borough records
Beverley: Possible scattered references.
Hedon: Alehouse recognizances 1758-1828; Register of innkeepers' licences 1757-1873.

1828 on: Inns, Public Houses and Beer Shops

Quarter Sessions records
Sessions Order Books, occasional refs mid-19th century onwards 1828-1971, incl some Kingston-upon-Hull premises; Appeal and Recognizance Books, occasional refs 1828-1971.

Other County records
County Licensing Ctee mins 1895-1951; County Confirming and Compensation Ctee mins 1952-7; County Lic Ctee annual reports (incomplete) 1906-1920; Files re compensation on specific premises *c.*1907-1929; General correspondence of Licensing Committee 1906, 1916, 1918-27.

Hedon Borough records
Register of innkeepers' licences 1757-1873. Reg of innkeepers' lics, ale and beer and exciseable liquor 1872-74.

Petty Sessions records: registers of licences
Bainton Beacon Division. 1872-1901, 1940-75..
Beverley Borough Division. 1904-64
Buckrose Division. 1919-70.
Dickering Division 1935-67.
Holme Beacon Division 1946-76.
Holderness North Division 1904-71.
Howdenshire Division. 1936-76.
North Hunsley Division. 1904-58.
South Hunsley Division. 1924-41, 1961-73.
Wilton Beacon Division, 1925-76.

Police records
Kingston-upon-Hull: Alehouse regs 1880-88, *c.*1900, 1928-39; Reg of lics *c.*1901-*c.*1902; Regs of transfers of alehouse lics 1909-42, 1948-69; Character of persons applying for alehouse lics 1886-92; Beer House regs 1885-1927; Beer House regs (On and Off licences) *c.*1899-*c.*1939.
Reg of lics (Beer Houses etc) *c.*1905-42; Transfer of Beer and Wine Off licences 1909-24, 1926-47; Character of persons applying for Beer and Wine Houses 1885-95; Character of persons applying for transfer of liquor lics 1885-87; Misc lics (billiard halls and off licences) 1911-28; Reports against licensed victuallers 1946-49.

Lower Goldcross Division: Constables' returns of innkeepers summoned to attend sessions 1849-1856; Lists of innkeepers 1849-58; Returns of retail beer lic lists from magistrate's clerk of Snaith district 1855-65; Innkeepers' lics; Summonses of delinquent innkeepers 1856-64.

Hull City Archives.

Hull Borough Records
Petty Sessions mins 1811-24.
Mins of lic meetings 1883-1952.
Rough brewster sessions mins 1908-09, 1912-41.
Lics extension books 1956-74.
Reg of lics 1905.
Reg of alehouses 1954-68, 1918-62.
Reg of beerhouses 1917-62.
Compensation authority mins. 1904-08, 1927-47.
Plans of PHs, C20.
Mins of lic & planning c'tee 1946-77.

YORKSHIRE: NORTH RIDING

National records: see under 'Yorkshire', page 49.

National records: see under 'Yorkshire', page 49.

North Yorkshire County Record Office, *Northallerton.*

1552-1828: Inns and Alehouses

North Riding Quarter Sessions records
Registers of alehouses and alehouse keepers' recognizances, returns of recognizances of licensed victuallers, 1774-1811, 1822-29.
Returns of alehouse keepers 1717-20.

1828 on: Inns, Public Houses and Beer Shops

North Riding Quarter Sessions records
Alehouse licensing ctee mins 1873-1942.

Petty Sessions records
Allertonshire: registers of licences 1937-67.
Birdforth: register of licences 1872-1973.
Gilling East: register of licences 1935-67.
Hang West: register of registered premises 1907-1929; register of licences 1903-20.
Langbaurgh East: list of inn licences granted 1850-1870; copies of register of Refreshment Houses and wine licences 1864-69; retail beer licence lists 1864-69; photographs of licensed premises n.d.
Langbaurgh West: register of licences 1903-66.
Pickering Lythe East: register of licences 1872-1948.

Teesside Archives, *Middlesbrough.*

Langbaurgh North: Reg of lics 1931-54; Lic mins 1928-36.
Middlesbrough: Reg of lics 1912-54.
Redcar and Saltburn: Reg of lics 1921-60.

YORKSHIRE: WEST RIDING

Boroughs which were their own licensing authority: Doncaster, Leeds.

Licensing Districts post-1828:
Agbrigg Lower, Barkston Ash Upper, Bingley, Brighouse Borough Division, Calder, Dewsbury, Keighley, Morley East, Osgoldcross Upper, Osett Borough Division, Otley, Pudsey Borough Division, Skyrack, Todmorden, Wetherby, Batley Borough, Bradford Borough, Dewsbury Borough, Halifax Borough, Leeds Borough, Morley Borough, Wakefield Borough.

> *National records:* see under 'Yorkshire', page 49.

> *West Yorkshire Archive Service H.Q., Wakefield.*

1552-1828: Inns and Alehouses

West Riding Quarter Session records
Sessions rolls and order books contain some references, rolls begin 1662, order books 1638.
Brewster sessions papers comprise lists of alehouse keepers arranged in wapentakes, submitted by petty constables 1693-1777.
Original recognizances 1752-1821, arranged under wapentakes.

Liberty of Ripon records
Borough and liberty sessions, alehouse recognizances 1770-1828.

1828 on: Inns, Public Houses and Beer Shops

West Riding Quarter Sessions records
Lic ctee mins 1872-1904, annual reports 1904-72; returns 1905.
Files concerning closure of premises and extinguishing of licences under 1904 Licensing Act, 1847-1968.
Compensation accounts 1905-48.
Liberty of Cawood, Wistow and Otley: beerhouse licensing, concerning value of property 1842-63.

West Riding Petty Sessions records
Registers of licensed alehouses: East Morley 1929-1955; Otley 1872-1972; Lower Agbrigg 1903-12, 1924-67; Wakefield 1872-1955; Ossett 1894-1972; Brighouse 1872-1974; Morley *c.*1893-1959; Skyrack 1902-72; Wetherby 1875-1971; Upper Barkston Ash 1904-55; Bradford *c.*1899-1969; Dewsbury 1873-1939, *c.*1958-*c.*1974; Upper Osgoldcross 1896-1963; Todmorden 1936-62; Halifax 1906-64; Calder 1895-1945; Pontefract 1939-72.
Registers of Store licences: East Morley 1897-1960; Keighley 1898-1954; Lower Agbrigg 1876-1946; Skyrack 1897-1974; Upper Osgoldcross 1915-74; Wetherby 1898-1964.
Other registers: Licensing court reg, Keighley 1975-1983; Reg of renewal of lics, Brighouse 1876-87; Reg of off-licences, Bradford 1899-1969; Reg of transferred licences, Bradford 1922-64; Reg of alterations to premises, Bradford 1886- 1955; Reg of plans submitted, Bradford 1955-72; Reg of beerhouses, Halifax 1906-60; Reg of off-licences, Calder 1895-1902.

West Riding Petty Sessions records continued
Alehouse plans: Keighley 1903-47; Lower Agbrigg 1960; Ossett *c.*1905-74.

Other Licences

West Riding Petty Session records
Music and dancing registers: Otley 1940-71; Pudsey 1962-72; Lower Agbrigg 1928-46; Wakefield 1892-1974; Ossett 1969-74; Brighouse 1893-96; Morley *c.*1950-*c.*1974; Calder 1954-77; Pontefract 1960-74.

See also *West Yorkshire Police Archives*, page 52.

> *Leeds District Archives.*

1552-1828: Inns and Alehouses

Leeds Borough Sessions records
Order books, 1698-1809, contain some general orders.

1828 on: Inns, Public Houses and Beer Shops

Leeds Borough records
Magistrates' minute books, 1826-1904, contain references to licensing matters, applications etc

Licences for other activities

Magistrates' minute books: music and dancing lics.

> *Kirklees District Archives, Huddersfield.*

Petition to sell beer, Meltham 1844 [KC312/16/1].
Brewer's licence, Almondbury 1883 [KC321/14/6].
Huddersfield County Borough, Police Force records: Reg of alehouses 1868-1965; Reg of beer sellers 1870-1965; Reg of transfers of intoxicating liquor lics 1879-1942.
Huddersfield County Borough Lic Ctee mins 1965-1974.

> *West Yorkshire Archaeological Service, Yorkshire Archaeological Service, Leeds.*

Notice to Swillington innkeeper re transfer of licence 1829 [MD 375].

> *Wakefield Library Headquarters, Wakefield.*

The John Goodchild Collection contains a few papers relating to applications for licences and also some Wakefield Borough papers relating to presentments of innholders, as well as much other material relating to inns and alehouses

> *Sheffield Archives, Sheffield.*

Magistrates' Court records
Upper Strafforth and Tickhill Div: Regs of off-licences 1872-96.
Sheffield Division: Regs of beerhouse keepers *c.*1870-*c.*1935 [microfilm A174-175]; Regs of lic'd victuallers *c.*1870-*c.*1935 [microfilm A174-175].
City of Sheffield Division: Precepts Book 1918-1935 incl dates and JPs for Special Licensing Sessions under 1910 Licensing Act.

Sheffield Wine and Beer Trade Association
Register of members 1887-1964.

Yorkshire: West Riding continued

Barnsley Archives & Local Studies Dept., Central Library, Barnsley.

Chief Constable's reports, Brewster Sessions 1907, 1926, contains lists of licensed premises and lists of extinct licences.

Barnsley Magistrates' Court, Petty Sessions.
Registers of licences 1889-95, 1922-58.
To view, a form first has to be collected at BA&LS, taken to the Court and signed for permission to view. This appears to be the only collection of such registers (in the public domain) requiring such restrictive access.

Doncaster Archives Department, Doncaster.

1552-1828: Inns and Alehouses

Doncaster Borough records
Lists of recogs 1631, 1635; Recogs 1802-05, 1808-1810; Calendared and indexed.

1828 on: Inns, Public Houses and Beer Shops

Magistrates' Court records
West Riding Division of Lower Strafforth and Tickhill, Doncaster Court, Regs of lics, 1886-1958; Doncaster Borough, Reg of licences, 1872-1961. Doncaster Magistrates' Court. On & Off lic regs 1962-81; Doncaster Borough reg of music & dancing reg, 1926-77.

Other licences

Music and dancing registers of licences:
West Riding Division of Strafford and Tickhill 1918-1945; Doncaster Borough 1911-31.

Rotherham M.B. Archives & Local Studies Section, Brian O'Malley Central Library.

Rotherham Magistrates' Court records
Court registers contain a few references to licensing matters, mainly transfers of licences, 19-20th cent.

North Yorkshire County Record Office, Northallerton.

Lower Barkston Ash: register of licences 1872-82; register of clubs 1903-39; annual club returns 1940-51; plans of proposed alterations to licensed premises 1902-53.
Ripon city: register of licences 1903-65.

East Riding of Yorkshire Archive Office, Beverley.

Petty Sessions records: registers of licences
Goole and Selby Division, c.1951-69. Includes entries for Lower Osgolcross Division, c.1951-55; also earlier entries 1914-51, possibly transferred into new register.
Lower Barkston Ash Division. 1910-55.
Lower Osgoldcross Division. 1901-51.

Lancashire County Record Office, Preston.

Petty Sessions records
Bolton by Bowland Division: Regs of alehouse lics 1883-98.

West Yorkshire Police Archives.

The records are all actually held at *the West Yorkshire Archives, Wakefield*. However, a letter of authority, quoting the reference number 'A113/25' with a short description, must first be obtained from The Archivist, Media & Public Relations Dept., West Yorkshire Police, PO Box 9, Wakefield WF1 3QP.
See also *A History of the Police in West Yorkshire*; and Colin Jackson, *Researching Police Ancestry in Yorkshire*, 1994 (published by the author, 34 Castle View, Sandal, Wakefield, West Yorks WF2 7HZ).

West Riding Constabulary
Register of refreshment house keepers, Halifax West Morley Division, 1857-1960.
Annual reports of brewster sessions, 1953-67.

Bradford City Police
Licensing registers, 23 vols, 1858-1975.

Leeds City Police
Reg of off-licences 1879-1910; reg of music lics 1890-1967; visits to lic'd premises 1956-63; transfers of liquor lics (3 vols) 1965-70; reg of shops and off-licences, 'A' Div, 1874-1952; regs of lics for public music, 'A' Div [no date]; reg of beer sellers 1860-90; reg of lic'd premises 1861-1913; reg of lic victuallers 1889-1952; reg of lic'd beer houses, 1892-1952; lic'd premises reports (3 vols) 1913-68; reg of cinemas, music and dancing 1923-1962; refreshment house book, 'B' Div, 1871-1900; annual reports of chief constable to brewster sessions 1881-1958; reg of lic'd premises (7 vols) 1874-1972.

WALES

Letters Patent (1554-71): see under counties.
Vintners' fines (1569-72): none.
Victuallers' (Lenten) Recognizances (1572-1634).
Raleigh Wine Licences (1583-1602): none.
Mompesson Licences (1620): see under counties.
Coventry Wine Licences (1626-49): see under counties.
Wine Licences: Pipe Office (1670-1756).
Military Survey 1756 (page 11): see under counties.

ANGLESEY

National Records (see pages 6-8)

Coventry Wine Licences (1634): Beaumaris.

Anglesey County Record Office, *Llangefni.*

Quarter Sessions, 1808-1897. Records including Order Books and later rolls may have references.
Petty Sessions. 1883-1924.

BRECONSHIRE

National Records (see pages 6-8)

Letters Patent (1554-71): Brecknock.
Coventry Wine Licences (1635): Brecknock.

National Library of Wales, *Aberystwyth.*

Petty Sessions records
Hundred of Crickhowell. Mins 1791-1815 [Castell Gorford 3] may contain refs to alehouse licences.

Powys County Archives Office, *Llandrindod Wells.*

Quarter Sessions records
Order books and sessions rolls include recognizances, presentments etc.

Petty Sessions records
Registers of licences: Brecon Division 1945-80; Builth Division 1932-86; Crickhowell Division 1950-1974; Defynnog Division 1950-68; Hay Division 1874--82, 1919-27, 1959-63; Merthyr and Pencelli Division 1935-68; Talgarth Division 1873-93, 1959-1963; Ystradgynlais Division 1919-60.

CAERNARVONSHIRE

National Records (see pages 6-8)

Coventry Wine Licences (1626/7): Pwlltheli.
Military Survey 1756 District: towns, signs, numbers of beds and stabling [WO 30/49, ff.151-52].

Caernarfon Record Office, *Caernarfon.*

1552-1828: Inns and Alehouses

Quarter Sessions records
Sessional rolls contain original recognizances.
Original recogs (kept separate) 1804, 1810, 1818, 1820-24; Recognizance Book 1626-28.

1828 on: Inns, Public Houses and Beer Shops

Quarter Sessions records
Lic ctee mins, applications for lics 1878-83, 1905-1932; Lic returns 1878-1881; Compensation papers 1901-32.

Petty Sessions records
Minute Books, regs and papers for all divisions from mid to late-19th century (with some gaps and not yet fully listed), which include licensing affairs.

CARDIGANSHIRE (Ceredigion)

National Records (see pages 6-8)

Coventry Wine Licences (1634): Cardigan.
Military Survey 1756 (see page 11). Cardigan and District: towns, innkeepers, signs, beds and stabling [WO 30/49, ff.151-52].

National Library of Wales, *Aberystwyth.*

Petty Sessions
Aberaeron Division and Lower Division of Hd of Ilar. Order book, 1817-24 [NLW MS 11488E].
Aberaeron. Mins [nd. NLW MSS 20887C, 13867-8E, 20887C] may contain refs to alehouse lics.
Penrhiwpal. Mins 1872-78; Llandysul. Mins 1926-29 [Amphlett Lewis and Evans Papers] may contain refs to alehouse lics.

Cardiganshire: *Cerdigion Archives* continued

Ceredigion Archives, Aberystwyth.

Cardiganshire Quarter Sessions records
Order books 1739-1971 [QS/OB/1-14] may contain
some references to licensing of alehouses.
Cardiganshire Licensing Committee, minutes 1905-
1938 [Cards/QS/L/1].

Petty Sessions
Regs of lics: Aberystwyth Division 1947-68;
Aberaeron Division 1957-71; Lampeter 1945-71;
Llanbadarn 1937-68 [TPS/LLB/1/13]; Llandyssul
1900-58; Llanilar 1889-1924, 1940-68; Talybont
1937-68.

CARMARTHENSHIRE

Licensing Divisions, post-1828:
Carmarthen Borough, Carmarthen Division,
Llanelli Division.

National Records (see pages 6-8)

Coventry Wine Licences (1629, 1635): Carmarthen,
Llandovery.
Military Survey 1756 (see page 11). Carmarthen
(Llandiloo District), places, victuallers, signs,
numbers of beds [WO 30/49, ff.147-48, 153-54].

Carmarthenshire Archives Service, Carmarthen.

1552-1828: Inns and Alehouses
Quarter Sessions records
Probably no licensing records, though the Order
Books may contain some references, 1748-52,
1794-1813, 1820-1971.

1828 on: Inns, Public Houses and Beer Shops

County records
Lic ctee mins and compensation papers, 1873-99,
1905-19.

Petty Sessions records
Regs of victuallers' lics: Carmarthen Division 1891-
1893, 1912-20; Carmarthen Borough 1872-83,
1891-1906; Llanelli Division 1893-1901, 1903-24.
Licensing returns: Carmarthen Division, 1894.

DENBIGHSHIRE

Boroughs which were their own licensing authority:
Denbigh, Ruthin.
Licensing Divisions, post-1828:
Bromfield, Colwyn, Denbigh, Isaled, Isdulas,
Llangollen and Upper Chirk/Ceiriog/Llansilin,
Ruabon, Ruthin, Uwchaled, Uwchdulus, Wrexham,
Wrecsam Maelor.

National Records (see pages 6-8)

Letters` Patent (1554-71): Denbigh.
Coventry Wine Licences (1629-37): Ruthin, Wrexham.

Denbighshire Record Office, Ruthin.

1552-1828: Inns and Alehouses

Quarter Sessions records
Sessional rolls, 1706-1971; Regs of victuallers,
1733-1823; Alehouse recogs, 1757, 1772-1828;
Petitions for lics, Ruthin borough, 1813-15.

Borough records
Mins of Denbigh Quarter Sessions, contain recogs,
1806-35; Original recogs, 1809, 1817-29.

1828 on: Inns, Public Houses and Beer Shops

Quarter Sessions
Licensing committee mins 1884-1952; agenda papers
1923-57; reg of extnguished lics 1905-39, 1955-6;
reg of lics referred for renewal 1905-9; county
returns of publica and beer houses, 1891, 1894,
1900, 1918-19; list of licensed premises, 1970.

Petty Sessions records
Bromfield Division: Regs of lics, 1872-97, 1901-53;
Court regs 1918-74; Ctee mins 1922-74.
Colwyn Bay, later Colwyn Division: Reg of lics 1934-
1962; Court regs 1954-81; Ctee mins 1954-82.
Denbigh Division; Reg of lics 1903-67; Court reg
1916-1974; Ctee mins 1907-23.
Isaled Division: Reg of lics 1914-62; Court regs
1907-74; Ctee mins 1893-1925.
Isdulas Division; Reg of lics 1872-1948; Court regs
1880-1974; Ctee mins 1867-1974.
Llangollen and Upper Chirk etc Division: Court reg
1942-59; Ctee mins 1874-1942.
Ruabon Division: Reg of lics 1872-1945; Court reg
1880-1974; Ctee mins 1896-1964.
Ruthin Division: Reg of lics 1924-67; Court reg 1915-
1974; Ctee mins 1910-37.
Uwchaled Division: Reg of lics 1962-7;Court reg
1924-1970.
Uwchdulas Division: Reg of lics 1934-67; Court reg
1909-70; Ctee mins 1910-72.
Wrexham Division: Reg of lics 1885-1953; Court reg
1889-1974; Ctee mins 1904-73.
Wrecsam Maelor Division: Court reg 1974- .

Flintshire Record Office, Hawarden.

1552-1828: Inns and Alehouses

Warrant re disorderly houses in Chirk Hundred 1658.

FLINTSHIRE

National Records (see pages 6-8)

Coventry Wine Licences (1626, 1634): Holywell, Northop.

Flintshire Record Office, *Hawarden.*

1552-1828: Inns and Alehouses

Quarter Sessions records
Sessional rolls, 1747-52 contains original recognizances.

1828 on: Inns, Public Houses and Beer Shops

Quarter Sessions records
Lic ctee mins, Flint 1872-9, 1901-3; draft mins 1905-1925.

1828 on continued

Petty Sessions records
Registers of licences: Flint 1897-1962; Hawarden 1955-71; Hope 1955-70; Mold 1953-71; Northop 1955-70; Overton 1906-1971; Prestatyn 1916-1963 Rhuddlan 1872-1964.

Flint Constabulary records
Returns of licensed houses, 1892, 1903.
Regs of licensed houses: Flint 1904-62; Hawarden, Hope and Mold 1901-62; Overton 1908-60.

Licences for other activities

Petty Sessions records
Music and dancing: Flint 1954-59; Hawarden, Hope etc 1955-74.

GLAMORGAN

National Records (see pages 6-8)

Coventry Wine Licences (1626-36): 'Aberhalve', Bridgend, Cardiff, Neath, Swansea.

Glamorgan Record Office, *Cardiff*
(serving Cardiff, Vale of Glamorgan, Merthyr Tydfil, Bridgend, Rhodda Cynon Taff, Caerphilly).

1552-1828: Inns and Alehouses

Quarter Sessions records
Register of alehouse recognizances 1753-63.
Alehouse keepers' recognizances 1823-27.

Borough records
Presentments of the grand jury of the town and liberty of Cardiff, including unlicensed alehouse keepers 1644, 1656/7.

1828 on: Inns, Public Houses and Beer Shops

Petty Sessions records
Caerphilly Higher Division: Lic regs, intoxicating liquor 1912-60.
Caerphilly Lower Division: Regs of lics 1872-1934.
Cardiff Borough: Lic court records 1938, 1967-74; General mins, 1857-1956, including mins of Lic Ctee

Glamorganshire: Glamorgan R.O. continued

before 1919; Lic Ctee mins 1919-57; Complaints of the Superintendent of Police against disorderly houses 1889-95.
Cowbridge Division: Reg of lics 1894-1911.
Dinas Powis Division: Reg of lics 1926-36.
Kibbor Division: Lic ctee mins 1959-67.
Merthyr Borough: Mins, including lic 1908-10, 1914-1920.
Miskin Higher Division: Lic regs, intoxicating liquor 1872-1960.
Miskin Higher and Caerphilly Higher Division: Lic book 1941-56.
Miskin Lower Division: Reg of lics 1869-1907, 1923-1943.
Newcastle and Ogmore Division: Reg of victualling houses 1866-69, 1903-28; Reg of lics 1959-62.

Police records
Glamorgan Constabulary: Pontycymmer police station: vol containing details of licensed premises and other matters 1959-67.
Cardiff Borough Police: Plans of licensed premises in Cardiff, mostly minor alterations 1897-1965; Chief Constable's annual reports to the licensing JPs with Licensing Calendar (statistics and list of applications) 1915-55, and reports to the Lic Ctee 1956-64; Regs of alehouses, beerhouses and grocers' lics Divisions B and C 1879-1965.
Merthyr Tydfil Borough Police: Chief Constable's Annual reports to the Licensing Ctee 1949, 1952-1968; Reg of alehouse lics 1960-68.
Swansea Borough Police: Chief Constable's Annual reports to the Licensing Ctee 1962, 1964-67.

Other licences

Petty Sessions records
Caerphilly Lower Division: Music and dancing lics reg 1915-47.
Miskin Lower Division: Reg of music and dancing 1893-1916, 1919-44.

Police records
Cardiff Borough Police: Music lics, including papers relating to applications from 'alehouses' 1940-66.

West Glamorgan Archive Service, *Swansea.*
(serving Swansea, Neath Port Talbot).

Petty Sessions records
Registers of licences: Aberavon 1903-38; Neath Hundred 1903-31; Neath Borough 1894-1962; Pontardawe 1903-29; Port Talbot Borough 1920-1941 and 1975-77; Swansea Hundred 1903-67; Swansea Borough 1881-1914 and 1946-62.
Commitee mins: Neath Hundred 1923-61.
Licensing files: Neath Borough 1921-53.
Other records, Swansea Borough: Record of lics refused and transferred 1903-19; Reg of transfers 1880-1915; Compensation authority mins 1914-1947; Reg of applications 1977-84; Mins 1932-57.

Other licences
Music and dancing lics: Neath Hundred 1930-55.

MERIONETH

National Records (see pages 6-8)

Coventry Wine Licences (1634): Aberdovey.

No locally held records notified.

MONMOUTHSHIRE (Gwent)

Boroughs which were their own licensing authority:
Monmouth.
Licensing Districts post-1828:
Abergavenny, Bedwellty, Chepstow, Monmouth
County, Monmouth Borough, Newport, Pontypool,
Trelleck, Usk.

National Records (see pages 6-8)

Coventry Wine Licences (1626-35): Abergavenny,
Chepstow, Magor, Monmouth, Newport, Usk and
Trostry.

Gwent Record Office, *Cwmbran*
(serving Monmouthshire, Newport, Torfaen, Blaenau
Gwent, Caerphilly).

1552-1828: Inns and Alehouses

Quarter Sessions records
Original recogs 1810-25; Government reports, 1811
onwards; Quarter Session mins incl alehouse
recognizances 1819-27 (see index 'licensing').

Borough records
Monmouth: Ale and victualling house recognizance
book, 1822; Lists of licenced houses 1830-35.

1828 on: Inns, Public Houses and Beer Shops

County records
County Lic Ctee mins and misc papers, 1873-1904;
County Lic confirming and compensation authority
mins 1904-73; Draft mins 1930-70; Treasurer's
account compensation fund 1905-27; Licensing
papers and correspondence, applications for lics,
licensing maps and plans etc 1872-1961.

Quarter Sessions records
Regs of lics (beer houses and wine certificates),
Bedwellty Division 1875-78.
Particulars of licensed houses 1904-05.
Regs of lics referred 1905-12.

Petty Sessions records
Register of lics (beer house and wine certificates):
Abergavenny Division 1915-74; Bedwellty Division
1872-1967; Monmouth County Division 1937-49 ;
Monmouth Borough Division 1881-1954; Newport
Borough Division 1872-1932; Pontypool Division
1885-1971; Trelleck Division 1906-52; Usk
Division 1932-54.
Plans of licensed houses, 312 named places
Pontypool Division.
Lists of licensed premises, Bedwellty Division 1939-
1946.

Monmouthshire continued

Licences for other activities

Regs of Music and Dancing: Abergavenny Division
1915-60; Newport Borough Division 1925-51.
Regs of billiards lics 1923-54.

MONTGOMERYSHIRE

National Records (see pages 6-8)

Coventry Wine Licences (1634-5): Machynlleth,
Welshpool.

Powys County Archives Office, *Llandrindod Wells.*

1552-1828: Inns and Alehouses

Quarter Sessions records
Order books and sessions rolls include
recognizances, presentments etc.

1828 on: Inns, Public Houses and Beer Shops

Quarter Sessions records
Licensing Ctee mins, correspondence etc 1903-34.

Petty Sessions records registers of licences:
Cawrse, 1911-1961.
Daytheur Division, 1929-73.
Llanfyllin Borough, 1903-57.
Llanfyllin and Pool Lower, 1927-36.
Llanfyllin Division, 1938-70.
Llanidloes Borough, 1903-57.
Llanidloes Lower, 1940-59.
Llanidloes Lower Division and Lalanfyllin, 1960-73.
Llanidloes Upper, 1914-60.
Llanidloes Upper Division and Borough, 1963-73.
Llanidloes Division, 1963-73.
Machynlleth Division, 1907-67, 1945-73, 1996-2002.
Matheral Division, 1907-67.
Montgomery Division, 1960-1973, 1996-2002.
Newtown Division, 1911-70, 1974.
Newtown Upper, 1880-94, 1896-1901, 1903-1953,
1996-2002.
Pool Upper, 1911-37.
Welshpool Division, 1902-1908, 1953-73.

PEMBROKESHIRE

Boroughs which were their own licensing authority: Haverfordwest

National Records (see pages 6-8)

Mompesson Licences (1620): Caerau, Pembroke, Tenby.

Military Survey 1756 (see page 11). Haverfordwest: places, victuallers, signs, number of beds, stabling [WO 30/49, ff.151-52]; Tenby District: places, victuallers and signs, number of beds [WO 30/49, ff.149-50].

Pembrokeshire Record Office, *Haverfordwest.*

1552-1828: Inns and Alehouses

Quarter Sessions records
Sessional rolls contain some original recognizances 1779 onwards.
Lists of licensed alehouse keepers, 1810-13.
Register of alehouse recognizances 1822-28.
Alehouse recognizances 1822-28.

Borough records
Town and county of Haverfordwest: Recogs and notices of applications, 1826; Sessional rolls for Michaelmas 1823-25 contain alehouse recogs.

1828 on: Inns, Public Houses and Beer Shops

Quarter Sessions records
Lic ctee mins/Compensation Authority mins, 1905-1961.
Plans and particulars, one or more licensed premises in following places, 1873-1910: Narberth, Robeston Wathen, Mynyddu, Lampeter Velfrey, St. Issells, Hakin, Maenclochog, Parrog in Newport Parish, Newport, Llandissilio, Solva, Milford Haven, Letterston, Goodwick, Herbrandston, Fishguard.
Licensing ctee papers, 1897-1900.
Memo from Licensed Victuallers' Central Board, 1906.
Financial statements required under 1910 Licensing Act, 1916-20.
Resolution of special meeting concerning hotel at Fishguard, 1910.
Rules made under 1949 Licensing Act.
Corres and reports, re renewal of licence, Portfield Gate inn, 1957.
Memo by the Licensed Victuallers' Central Board, 1906.

Published

Keith Johnson, *The pubs of Pembroke, Pembroke Dock, Tenby & South Pembrokeshire* (2003); *The Pubs of Narberth, Saundersfoot & South-East Pembrokeshire* (2004); *The Pubs of Havrefordwest, Milford Haven & Mid-West Pembrokeshire* (2006); Logaston Press.

RADNORSHIRE

National Records (see pages 6-8)

Letters Patent (1554-71): 'Radnorshire' (no place named).

Powys County Archives Office, *Llandrindod Wells.*

1552-1828: Inns and Alehouses

Quarter Sessions records
Order books and sessions rolls include recognizances, presentments etc.

1828 on: Inns, Public Houses and Beer Shops

Quarter Sessions records
Licensing Ctee mins, correspondence etc 1905-51.

Petty Sessions records
Registers of licences:
   Colwyn Division 1939-86;
   East Radnor Division 1959-86;
   Knighton Divison 1933-93
   Llandrindod Division 1913-51;
   Llandrindod Wells Divsion 1951-86;
   New Radnor Division 1915-1993;
   Painscastle Divsion 1923-27, 1935-86;
   Presteigne Division 1940-77;
   Rhayader Divsion 1954-86.

SCOTLAND

These records are arranged according to the way in which they are held and catalogued, rather than attempting to fit them into the English pattern.

National Archives of Scotland, Edinburgh.

Burgh Records
Burntisland: Licensing court record, 1756-1809.
Dunbar: Licensing court books, 1828-1902; scroll minutes 1954-75.
Inverurie: Ale certificate register 1847-53; Licence certificate register 1854-1912.
Musselburgh: Licensing court books, 1716-1975.
North Berwick: Reg of applications and court book, 1828-1975; Reg of places of public refreshment 1916-70.
Tranent: Reg of places of public refreshment 1913-1940.
See also under Counties, below.

Justice of the Peace records - licensing courts
County of Argyll: Ale licences 1778-93; reg of applications for publicans' certificates, Kintyre district, 1858-1901.
County of Banff: Licensing court book 1769-1828.
County of Berwick: Licensing court book, Ayton, 1854-74.
County of Caithness: Mins of licensing court (2 items) 1798 ; Licence to Isabel Ross of Thurso, 1810.
County of Dumfries: Mins 1876-1904; Reg of lics 1854-1904; Reg of applications 1904-20; Court book, Thornhill, 1854-90; Reg 1877-88.
East Lothian: Record of ale lics 1804-10; Reg of applications for lics 1832-40.
East Lothian County Council (f'ly Haddingtonshire), and predecessors: Licensing records 1825-1982.
City of Edinburgh: Mins, QS and lic courts, 1843-1902; Mins, PS and lic courts 1902-56.
County of Inverness: Court Books, Portree, 1836-1868; Application for liquor licences, Portree 1831-59 ; Excise licences roll 1858-77.
County of Kirkcudbright: Regs of application for lics Castle Douglas District 1855-1922; Creetown District 1861-1902; Kirkcudbright District 1849-1904; Burgh of Kirkcudbright 1865-1903; Maxwelltown District 1849-72; New Galloway District 1866-1902; Burgh of New Galloway 1885-1904.
County of Midlothian: Regs of application and renewal of lics 1828-1959; Reg of transfers of licences 1828-52; Lic court mins, 1904-47; Licensing court agenda book, 1913-62.
County of Peebles: Mins, QS, licensing oaths etc 1758-1974; Regs of applications for publicans' certs 1828-73.

National Archives of Scotland continued

Justice of the Peace records - licensing courts ctd.
County of Roxburgh: Reg of applications for lic certs 1871-1921 ; Reg of applications for lic cert Jedburgh 1883-1903; Reg of applications for lic cert Hawick 1894-1904; Reg of applications for lic cert Kelso 1893-1904; Ale lic regs 1828-54.
County of Sutherland: QS mins, incl lic courts, 1901-1923; Regs of applications for publicans' certs 1839-1902.
County of West Lothian: reg of applications for ale licences 1854-74; applocationd 1899-1944.

Strathclyde Regional Archives Office, Mitchell Library, Glasgow.

Records of the Justices of the Peace
County of Dumbarton: Mins, incl QS, Ordinary and licensing courts, 1727-1975.
County of Renfrew: Reg of liquor licences granted, Paisley 1859-1922.
County of Lanark: Lic court books, 1830-96; Lic ctee mins 1876-1903

Shetland Archives Office, Lerwick.

Justice of the Peace records
County of Zetland: Reg of applications for certs 1828-39; Reg of applications for publicans' certs 1839-79; Reg of applications for the sale of exiseable liquors 1880-1962; Bundle of convictions 1857-79; Petition to licensing court from Unst, n.d.; Petition from Burgh of Lerwick, 1921; Licensed premises plans, 1906.

St Andrew's University Library.

Burgh records
Cupar: Record of ale licences 1828-1902.
Earlsferry: Licensing register 1901-03.
Newburgh: Certs for exciseable liquors 1854-1904.
St. Andrews: Licensing Court records.

Kyle and Carrick District Offices.

Burgh records
Ayr: Ale licence book 1785-1828; Register of applications for publicans' certs 1828-1900.

Clydesdale District Council Offices, Lanark.

Burgh records
Lanark: JP lic court books 1830-96; Reg of applications to licensing court 1897-1939.

City Chambers, Edinburgh.

Burgh records
Edinburgh: Regs of ale certs 1775-1828 and later.

Statutes concerned with licensing retailers of ale, beer, wine, spirits and non-alcholic beverages

For the text of the Acts consult the various volumes of *Statutes at Large*.

1552 An Act for keepers of alehouses to be bound. 5/6 Edward VI c25.

1553 An Act to avoid the excessive price of wine. 7 Edward VI c5.

1623 An Act concerning monopolies. 21 James I c3.

1627 An Act for the better suppressing of unlicensed alehouse keepers. 3 Charles I c4.

1660 For the better selling of wines by retail and for preventing abuses in mingling, corrupting and vitiating of wine and for the settling and limiting the prices of the same. 12 Charles II c25.

1663 An additional Act for the better ordering and collecting the duty of excise. 15 Charles II c11.

1663 For settling the profit of the Post Office and the power of granting wine licences on his Royal Highness the Duke of York. 15 Charles II c14.

1671 For revesting the power of granting wine licences in his Majesty, his heirs and successors and for setting a recompense on his Royal Highness ... in lieu thereof. 22/23 Charles II c6.

1701 For granting to His Majesty several duties upon low wines or spirits of the first extraction.12/13 William III c11.

1701 For encouraging the consumption of malted corn and for the better preventing the running of French and brandy. 1 Anne Session 2 c14.

1710 For licensing and regulating hackney coaches and chairs, ... and for securing ... a weekly payment out of the Post Office, and by several duties on hides and skins. 9 Anne c23.

1719 For preventing frauds and abuses in the public revenues of excise, stamp duties, post office, and house money. 6 George I c21.

1725 For granting an aid to His Majesty and by laying a duty upon victuallers and retailers of ale and beer within the cities of London and Westminster and the weekly bills of mortality. 12 George I c12.

1729 For laying a duty upon compound waters or spirits and for licensing the retailers thereof. 2 George II c17.

1729 An Act to revive the laws therein mentioned relating to the importation of foreign brandy and other waters and spirits,.... for the more effectual debarring of unlawful games; for licensing retailers of brandy and other distilled liquors, and for the better regulation of licences for common inns and alehouses. 2 George II c28.

1733 An Act for repealing an Act for laying a duty on compound waters or spirits and for licensing the retailers thereof, and for determining certain duties on French brandy, and for granting other duties in lieu thereof, and for enforcing the laws for preventing the running of brandies. 6 George II c17.

1736 An Act for laying a duty upon the retailers of spirituous liquors and for licensing the retailers thereof. 9 George II c23.

1737 For repealing the present duty on sweets, and for granting a less duty thereupon; and enforcing the execution of an act passed in the ninth...An Act for laying a duty upon the retailers of spirituous liquors, and for the licensing the retailers thereof; ... [licensing sweets]. 10 George II c17.

1737 For the more effectual preventing of unlawful playing of interludes within the precincts of the two Universities ... and for explaining and amending so much of [9 George II c23] ... as may affect the privileges of the two Universities with respect to licensing taverns and all other public houses within the same. 10 George II c19.

1743 For repealing certain duties on spirituous liquors and on licences for retailing the same, and for laying other duties on spirituous liquors and on licences to retail the said liquors. 16 George II c8.

1743 For repealing the several rates and duties upon victuallers and retailers of beer and ale, within the cities of London and Westminster and the weekly bills of mortality, and for the transferring the exchequer bills unsatisfied thereupon, to the duties for licences to sell spirituous liquors and strong waters by retail, and also for enabling his Majesty to raise a certain sum of money for the service of one year 1743, to be further charged on the said duties for licences. 16 George II c12.

1747 For granting a duty to His Majesty, to be paid by distillers, upon licences taken out by them for retailing spirituous liquors. 20 George II c39.

1751 For granting to His Majesty an additional duty upon spirituous liquors, and upon licences for retailing the same; and for repealing the Act of the 20th year of his present Majesty's reign An Act for granting a duty ... and for the more effectual restraining the retailing of distilled spirituous liquors; and for allowing a drawback upon the exportation of British made spirits. 24 George II c40

1753 An Act for the more effectually preventing the fraudulent removal of tobacco by land or water and for the ease of the fair trader in tobacco; and for ascertaining the rates payable for the portage of certain letters; and for amending and explaining the laws relating to the sale of spirituous liquors by retail.
26 George II c13.

1753 For the regulating the manner of licensing ale-houses in that part of Great Britain called England and for the more easy convicting persons selling ale and other liquors without licence. 26 George II c31.

1755 For making perpetual an Act passed in the 25th year of the reign of His Majesty for the better preventing of thefts and robberies, and for regulating places of public entertainment, and punishing persons keeping disorderly houses; for the further punishing persons selling ale or other liquors without licence.
28 George II c19.

1756 For granting to His Majesty a duty upon licences for retailing beer and ale and other excisable liquors and for establishing a method for granting such licences in Scotland, And for allowing such licences to be granted at petty session in England in a certain case therein mentioned.
29 George II c12.

1757 For granting to His Majesty several rates and duties upon indentures, leases, bonds ... and upon upon licences for retailing wine.
30 George II c19.

1828 Alehouse Act.
1830 Beer House Act.
1834 Beer House Act.
1860 Refreshment and Wine Licences Act.
1869 Wine and Beerhouse Act.
1872 Licensing Act.
1902 To amend the law relating to the sale of intoxicating liquors and to drunkenness.
1904 Compensation Act.
1908 Childrens Act.
1910 Licensing (Consolidation) Act.
1921 Licensing Act.

Glossary of Latin and English Words more or less synonymous with Inn and Public House or with Innkeeper, Publican etc.

Latin words and terms

The meanings are taken from *Dictionary of Medieval Latin from British Sources* by D. R. Howlett (Oxford 1989).

Brasiatores: brewers.

Caupo: tavern, inn.
Cauponia: tavern, tapstress.
Cauponius: taverner.
Cauponula: small tavern.

Domus tipliconis: tippling house/alehouse.

Eabulus: alehouse.

Hospes: innkeeper
Hospitalitas: inn; other meanings of the word include: hospitality, hospice, entertainment for guests, hospital for poor, sick and old.
Hospitator: innkeeper.
Hospitissa: hostess of an inn.
Hospitium: inn; other meanings of same word: hospitality, temporary lodging, eg billeting, guest house, hall of residence, hostel, hospice, Hospital of Knights of Order of St. John, dwelling house, residence for occasional use in town.

Taberna cervisiaria: alehouse.
Taberna vinaria: tavern (wine).
Taberna cauponaria: inn.
Tappatores or *tiplatores:* alehousekeepers.

English words and terms

In use during Tudor and early Stuart periods

Alehouse: a house selling ale and beer for consumption on, and perhaps off, the premises. Food was also usually sold.
Alehouse keeper: person in charge of an alehouse

Aqua vitae house: a house selling spirits: there is a reference to one at Barking in 1572, and to aqua vitae men (retailers) in Wiltshire in 1584.

Boosing ken: thieves' cant for an alehouse.
Brewer: common brewer: person who brewed ale for sale by retail and also to alehouses and inns.

Cannyker: a Norfolk word meaning alehouse or tippling house.
Common tables: houses referred to by this term probably provided set meals to be consumed on the premises, and would not have been alehouses.

Gannokers: City of Norwich mayor's proclamation, mid-fifteenth century (see *cannyker*).

English words and terms *continued*

Herbergeours: person in charge of an inn without stable accommodation, term probably obsolete by Tudor period.
Hostelry: this may, or may not, be a term for a slightly different establishment from an inn.

Abbeys and other religious houses usually had a guest house (hospitium) which provided free food and lodging for travellers and it is possible that these were known as hostelries as against inns which charged for accommodation.

One example found of the term 'petty hostelries' clearly meaning alehouses.
Host: person in charge of an inn.
Hosteller: person in charge of a hostelry or inn.

Inn: in all its various meaning (until recent times) the word inn includes the idea of lodging — be it for students, private people using their own inn, or for travellers. The main purpose of the public or common inn was to provide lodgings and refreshment for its guests. It is likely that the idea of inns providing food and drink for people not staying at the inn was not yet a generally accepted practice during the Middle Ages. This was the business of the other establishments—taverns, alehouses, cookshops and other victualling houses.

Tudor and Stuart inns sometimes included a tavern, a separate room selling wine to all comers, rather like a public bar in a modern hotel.

In the sixteenth and seventeenth centuries, and more so in later periods, the word was sometimes carelessly used to include alehouses. On the other hand eighteenth and early nineteenth century trade directories frequently differentiated between inns and hotels, and public houses.

Today the word still retains its original meaning of a place with lodgings for travellers, but it is also used to mean an old public house, particularly one in a country village or town centre.

Innholder or *innkeeper:* person in charge of an inn.

Ordinary: a term used for a set meal in an inn or tavern, and also for a house providing meals at a set price which was neither an inn nor tavern — a restaurant.

Post house: an inn or other house where horses were kept ready for the royal couriers (1511-1635) and where post boys and post horses were kept ready to despatch the mail to the next post house, and to take and guide travellers at a rapid pace.

During the coaching era the term came to mean a high class inn which provided post horses and post chaise for hire.

Pot house: a derogatory term for an alehouse.

Tavern: this term would appear to be restricted to houses selling wine during the Middle Ages and Tudor and Stuart periods. Food was often sold at the tavern.

Samuel Johnson defined a tavern as a house specialising in the sale of wine, but by the late eighteenth century there were few such taverns outside London, and the term had fallen out of use as a description of a wine house; it had come to be an alternative word for public house, a house that sold beer, spirits and wine.

Taverner: person in charge of a tavern.

Tippling house: this may be merely an alternative word for alehouse or may indicate a small alehouse or one not selling any food. It was used as early as 1308 in a custumal of the City of Norwich. The term fell out of use in the late seventeenth century.

Tippler, typler: person in charge of a tippling house, an alehouse keeper.

In Rye the term was used for anyone selling ale or beer and therefore liable for a quarterly tax.

Victualling houses: it is possible that this term sometimes referred to eating-houses, but in numerous documents it clearly is more or less synonymous with 'alehouse'. The phrase may also sometimes be used simply as a cover-all term for all kinds of houses and shops selling food and drink.

Victualler: a person providing food and drink. In many documents the term is used as synonymous with alehouse keeper, but sometimes it was used to cover all traders involved in the food trade.

There is also the more specialised meaning of the word: a person supplying food to the army or navy.

Vintner: a merchant dealing in wine; in many cases the person referred was also a wine retailer.

Vitler: an alternative spelling for victualler.

Wine drawer, wine retailer: person in charge of a tavern, or selling wine in an inn.

Note. The following terms appear to go out of use by or during the latter half of the seventeenth century: Cannyker, Common tables, Gannokers, Herberge-ours, Tippling house, Tippler/typler, Vitler, Wine drawer.

Words which came into use during the late Stuart and Hanovarian periods

Brandy shop: a house specialising in the sale of brandy and other spirits, though it may also have sold other beverages.

Chocolate house: a house specialising in the sale of chocolate and other non-alcoholic drinks, though it was likely to have also sold other beverages, including spirits.

Coffee house: a house specialising in the sale of coffee and other non-alcoholic drinks, though it is likely to have also sold other beverages, including spirits, wine, ale and beer. Some houses which were called coffee houses were nothing more than alehouses whose keepers were offering more than ale and beer.

Coffee man: this was the term used for the 'landlord' of a coffee house in the seventeenth century.

Dram shop: a house specialising in the sale of spirits, though it may have also sold other beverages.

Gin shop: this term would appear to be rarely used for a house specialising in the sale of spirits in the eighteenth century. It became the general term for such retail outlets in the 1820s.

Hot water house: a house specialising in the sale of spirits (hot water).

Mug house: an alehouse where the customers' mugs were displayed.

Mum house: an alehouse specialising in the sale of mum, a beer popular in the seventeenth century.

Post house: a good quality inn where post horses could be hired. In the latter half of the seventeenth century this was likely to be an inn which was also a post office. By the mid-eighteenth century other inns were offering this service, and also the hire of post chaise.

Postmaster: the innkeeper or other who ran the post office. The term was also used in the nineteenth century for an innkeeper or other who hired out postchaise and posthorses.

Postboy: 1. The inn servant (or employee of the postmaster) who carried the mail.
2. The inn servant who rode with the posthorses and postchaise and acted as guide.

Public house: a house licensed to sell ale, beer, and spirits, and maybe also wine. The term first came into use in the late seventeenth century, partly as an alternative term for alehouse, being a contraction of the term 'public alehouse'. However, the term was not exclusively used for alehouses, but could include small inns and taverns.

Punch house: a house specialising in the sale of punch, though it was likely also to sell other beverages.

Spirit shop: a house specialising in the sale of spirits.

Terms which came into general use after the 1750s

Beer shop/house: a house with a licence to sell beer, but not wine or spirits. Between 1830 and 1869 such houses did not need a licence from the magistrates' court, merely one issued by the local excise office.

Beer retailer: licensee of a beer shop.

Free house: a public house not tied to a brewery.

Gin palace: gin shop or public house with a very showey type of architecture.

Hotel: in the late eighteenth and early nineteenth century the term implied a better class of inn, a place providing accommodation and meals. Later in the nineteenth century it came to be used for unlicensed houses as well as public houses with sleeping accommodation.

Hush shop: unlicensed alehouse.

Local: a twentieth century colloquial term for the neighbourhood public house.

Motel: a hotel for motorists.

Off-licence: Over the centuries alehouses usually sold beer to be taken off the premises as well as for drinking in the alehouse. However, the 1830 Beer Act introduced a special licence for houses which *only* sold beer to be bought and taken away to drink.

Pub: a modern slang term for a public house; first recorded in 1865.

Road house: a superior public house catering for the motorist, particularly in the 1920s and '30s.

Tap: 1. A room within an inn where liquor is served, more or less equivalent to a public bar.
2. A public house within or attached to an inn, often with a separate licence.

Tom and Jerry Shops: a nickname for disorderly beer shops.

Wine lodge: a public house specialising in the provision of good quality wine.

Wine and spirit merchants: a public house, or more frequently an off-licence, specialising in the sale of spirits and wine.

For further reading

Lord Asquith, *Taverns, Their History and Laws.*
Peter Clark, *The English Alehouse: A Social History 1200-1830,* 1983.
Anthony Fletcher, *Reform in the Provinces: the Government of Stuart England,* 1986.
Simon Fowler, *Researching Brewery and Publican Ancestors,* 2009.
  This provides a more extensive and up-to-date bibliography.
Mark Girouard, *The Victorian Pub,* 1975. Mostly London.
Basil Oliver, *The Renaissance of the Public House.*

Inns have always been of interest and importance to local historians, so there are many histories of individual pubs, some good, some not so good. Little attempt has been made to refer to these (but see Simon Fowler's *Researching...,* above). However, the compilers can, for obvious reasons, recommend the following as examples:

Jeremy Gibson, 'A Century of Tavern-Keeping: 1. The Stokes Family at the Unicorn and Three Tuns [Banbury]', '2. The Three Tuns in the Eighteenth Century', *Cake & Cockhorse* (Banbury Historical Society), **7**.4 (Autumn 1977), **8**.1 (Autumn 1979); and B.S. Trinder and J.S.W. Gibson, 'Living in Banbury 1660-1730', *C&CH* **10**.9 (Summer 1988) for an inventory of the contents of the Three Tuns in 1722.
Judith Hunter, *George Inn [Southwark], London: An illustrated souvenir,* The National Trust, 1989.